The Development of Western Civilization

*Narrative Essays in the History of Our Tradition from
Its Origins in Ancient Israel and Greece to the Present*

Edited by Edward W. Fox
*Professor of Modern European History
Cornell University*

THE AGE OF RECOVERY
The Fifteenth Century

By JERAH JOHNSON

and WILLIAM A. PERCY, JR.

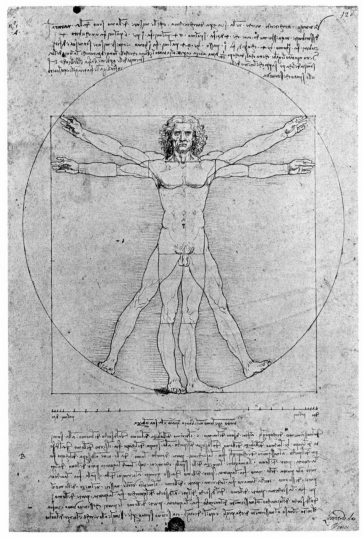

Leonardo da Vinci, *Vitruvian Man*, 1485–1490.
Galleria dell' Academia, Venice

THE

AGE OF RECOVERY

The Fifteenth Century

JERAH JOHNSON

LOUISIANA STATE UNIVERSITY,
NEW ORLEANS

AND

WILLIAM A. PERCY, JR.

UNIVERSITY OF MASSACHUSETTS,
BOSTON

Cornell University Press

ITHACA AND LONDON

First published 1970

Standard Book Number 8014-9858-9
Library of Congress Catalog Card Number 76-108161

PRINTED IN THE UNITED STATES OF AMERICA
BY VAIL-BALLOU PRESS, INC.

Foreword

THE proposition that each generation must rewrite history is more widely quoted than practiced. In the field of college texts on Western civilization, the conventional accounts have been revised, and sources and supplementary materials have been developed; but it is too long a time since the basic narrative has been rewritten to meet the rapidly changing needs of new college generations. In the mid-twentieth century such an account must be brief, well written, and based on unquestioned scholarship and must assume almost no previous historical knowledge on the part of the reader. It must provide a coherent analysis of the development of Western civilization and its basic values. It must, in short, constitute a systematic introduction to the collective memory of that tradition which we are being asked to defend. This series of narrative essays was undertaken in an effort to provide such a text for an introductory history survey course and is being published in the present form in the belief that the requirements of that one course reflected a need that is coming to be widely recognized.

Now that the classic languages, the Bible, the great historical novels, even most non-American history, have dropped out of the normal college preparatory program, it is imperative that a text in the history of European civilization be fully self-explanatory. This means not only that it must begin at the beginning, with the origins of our civilization in ancient Israel and Greece, but that it must introduce every name or event that takes an integral place in the account and ruthlessly delete all others no matter how firmly imbedded in historical protocol. Only thus simplified and complete will the narrative present a sufficiently clear outline of those major trends and developments that have led from the beginning of our recorded time to the most pressing of our current problems. This simplification, however, need not involve intellectual dilution or evasion. On the contrary, it can effectively raise rather than lower the level of presentation. It is on this assumption that the present series has been based, and each contributor has been urged to write for a mature and literate audience. It is hoped, therefore, that the essays may also prove profitable and rewarding to readers outside the college classroom.

The plan of the first part of the series is to sketch, in related essays, the narrative of our history from its origins to the eve of the French Revolution; each is being written by a recognized scholar and is designed to serve as the basic reading for one week in a semester course. The developments of the nineteenth and twentieth centuries will be covered in a succeeding series which will provide the same quantity of reading material for each week of the second semester. This scale of presentation has been adopted in a conviction that any understanding of the central problem of the preservation of the integrity and dignity of the individual human being depends first on an examination of the origins of our tradition in the politics and philosophy of the ancient Greeks and the religion of the ancient Hebrews and then on a relatively more detailed knowledge of its recent development within our industrial urban society.

The decision to devote equal space to twenty-five centuries and to a century and a half was based on the analogy with the human memory. Those events most remote tend to be remembered in least detail but often with a sense of clarity and perspective that is absent in more recent and more crowded recollections. If the roots of our tradition must be identified, their relation to the present must be carefully developed. The nearer the narrative approaches contemporary times, the more difficult and complicated this becomes. Recent experience must be worked over more thoroughly and in more detail if it is to contribute effectively to an understanding of the contemporary world.

It may be objected that the series attempts too much. The attempt is being made, however, on the assumption that any historical development should be susceptible of meaningful treatment on any scale and in the realization that a very large proportion of today's college students do not have more time to invest in this part of their education. The practical alternative appears to lie between some attempt to create a new brief account of the history of our tradition and the abandonment of any serious effort to communicate the essence of that tradition to all but a handful of our students. It is the conviction of everyone contributing to this series that the second alternative must not be accepted by default.

In a series covering such a vast sweep of time, few scholars would find themselves thoroughly at home in the fields covered by more than one or two of the essays. This means, in practice, that almost every essay should be written by a different author. In spite of apparent drawbacks, this procedure promises real advantages. Each contributor will be in a position to set higher standards of accuracy and insight in an essay encompassing a major portion of the field of his life's work than could ordinarily be expected in surveys of some ten or twenty centuries. The inevitable discontinuity of style and interpretation could be modified by editorial coordination; but it was felt that some discontinuity was in itself desirable. No illusion is more easily acquired by the student in an elementary course, or is more prejudicial to the efficacy of such a course, than that a single smoothly articulated text represents the very substance of history itself. If the shift from author to author, week by week, raises difficulties for the beginning student, they are difficulties that will not so much impede his progress as contribute to his growth.

In this essay, *The Age of Recovery: The Fifteenth Century*, Mr. Jerah Johnson and Mr. William A. Percy, Jr., recount the gradual but accelerating reversal of the downward economic and demographic trends that had marked the history of the preceding century. Buoyed by a rising tide of population and prosperity, Europeans once more resumed what might be called their offensive against the limits of their knowledge, understanding, and control of their geographic environment and of their cultural heritage. For many historical observers the culmination of this effort came in the Italian Renaissance, with its unrivaled accomplishments in the fields of arts and letters. For others the crowning achievement was not merely the discovery of the New World, but the emergence of a new cosmology. For the authors of this essay, however, these spectacular accomplishments are part of an even larger story: that of the expansion of Europe geographically to the east as well as to the west, and intellectually through the recovery of the past, as well as by the development of a new concept of man and his potentialities. It is an awe-inspiring subject: the coming of age, the readiness to accept responsibility for his own fate, of western man as we know him today.

The authors and the editor wish to thank Mrs. Esther G. Dotson, Otakar Odlozilik, Steven Runciman, and Joseph R. Strayer for many useful suggestions.

EDWARD WHITING FOX

Ithaca, New York
January 1970

Contents

Maps

THE AGE OF RECOVERY
The Fifteenth Century

Introduction

IN the course of the fifteenth century Europe experienced a recovery that has seemed to many a miraculous rebirth. The century opened at a time of destitution and depression in which the very survival of western civilization appeared to be threatened. Plagues, wars, and famines ravaged a society already racked by economic dislocation, ecclesiastical corruption, and political disintegration. Europeans, however, not only succeeded in restoring order, stability, and prosperity, but they also embarked upon a series of astonishing undertakings which vastly extended their artistic, intellectual, and geographic horizons.

Indeed, some of their achievements, notably those of the Italian humanists, were so dazzling that subsequent views of the century have been distorted. Looking back from later periods, historians have tended to treat each of these accomplishments separately—the great discoveries, the commercial revolution, Italian humanism, the artistic revival, or the new monarchies—rather than treat them all as integral parts of the development of European civilization as a whole. The culmination of this approach, and of the uncritical enthusiasm it engendered, was the work of the great nineteenth-century historian Jakob Burckhardt. (See his *Civilization of the Renaissance in Italy*, 1860.) Europe, he asserted, underwent a cultural rebirth —a "Renaissance"—in the fifteenth century, particularly in Italy, which reawakened mankind from its long mediaeval night of religious obscurantism to resume its triumphal march toward intellectual and artistic emancipation.

More recently this formulation has come under the attack of scholars who argue that the Middle Ages were far less dark and the Renaissance far less revolutionary than Burckhardt had contended. Many of the "great innovations," they insist, were mere modifications of mediaeval antecedents, while important mediaeval institutions and attitudes survived well into the seventeenth and even eighteenth centuries. Modern historians are learning, however, that both change and continuity can be discerned in any century and that every age is in a sense a "period of transition." As a result, the whole concept of a "Renaissance" has come under suspicion, and some urge that it should be abandoned altogether. Others restrict the use of the term to designate styles in art and letters or simply to refer to a period of time, specifically the fifteenth century in Italy. This scholarly pruning of Burckhardt's theories has unquestionably improved our picture of the period, but pushed to its logical conclusion of exorcising the concept of a "Renaissance" completely, it produces a misconception quite as great as that which it is intended to correct.

Ultimately the "Renaissance" cannot be eliminated, simply because a cultural rebirth was consciously experienced, nurtured, and proclaimed by a small but extraordinary elite of Italian intellectuals. These men of letters, artists, and scholars believed they were engaged in launching a great revival of classical culture during the fifteenth century. It was they who first divided western history into three periods: ancient, mediaeval, and modern. By thus deliberately separating themselves from their immediate predecessors, whom they dismissed as "Gothic," they sought to rescue the classical tradition from the neglect and misunderstanding it had suffered during the preceding "Dark Ages." The fact that both man and nature had been distrusted, if not openly condemned, by most thinkers from St. Augustine in the fourth century to St. Bonaventura in the thirteenth, did not deter the men of the Renaissance from announcing as their goal the creation of a better world through the unlimited development of human potentiality and the uninhibited understanding and enjoyment of nature.

This essay, recounting the revival of Europe during the fifteenth century, employs the word "Renaissance" in its several current senses, depending upon the context. While it notes the spectacular accomplishments of individuals that have traditionally dominated historical accounts, it also attempts, by placing these achievements in a larger framework, to call attention to more mundane but still important matters. Thus it opens with a review of the state of European civilization at the beginning of the century and continues with an account of the regeneration of the long-stagnant economy by such factors as the growth of population, trade, and capital. Like the preceding economic depression, this revival profoundly affected the development of political and social institutions. In the urbanized West it tended to benefit both the bourgeoisie and the peasantry at the expense of the nobility, while in the East it favored the aristocrats, who began to consolidate their domination over the rapidly multiplying agrarian population. The new centralized bureaucracies of the western monarchies were able to subdue feudal forces and subordinate local interests. In central Europe, however, where centuries of struggle gravely impaired the authority of pope and emperor, the economic recovery was not sufficiently sustained or vigorous to permit the rebuilding of strong central institutions, and towns and lords generally retained their independence. East of the Elbe, where there were few towns, the efforts of lords to reduce their peasants to serfdom went unchallenged. Beyond the eastern rim of Europe, both the Ottoman sultans and the Muscovite tsars solidified their conquests, creating sprawling despotic empires of a non-western type.

Supported and encouraged by this economic and political revival, the artists and scholars of the age set out to create a new culture from the recently recovered remains of classic civilization without realizing that they were also incorporating many remains of the very mediaeval synthesis they intended to demolish. But in spite of this and the fact that in other areas of intellectual endeavor conscious efforts to defend and shore up traditions and institutions of the fourteenth century continued, the Renaissance drive to generate vibrant new styles and ideas as well as to exercise new authority or conquer new lands eventually produced a prosperous, proud, and powerful Europe that was significantly new in its determination and ability to assert its dominion over the entire world.

CHAPTER I

Economic and Social Changes〜〜〜〜

DURING the first half of the fifteenth century the horsemen of the Apocalypse—Conquest, Slaughter, Famine, and Plague—continued to ravage Europe. Except for the sparsely settled areas of the East, Europe appeared to be condemned to permanent economic depression and its consequent social, religious, and political chaos; but after approximately 1450, war and plague subsided, with the result that population increased and towns grew. This expansion of the market for food stimulated first agriculture and then trade in general, ultimately reviving and expanding the long-stagnant circulation of money. By the end of the century the economy was experiencing the unprecedented boom that would provide the wealth to send Columbus across the Atlantic, settle colonies in the Americas, and at the same time support a brilliant cultural revival at home.

This essay explains these dramatic achievements in terms of a major rise in population that reversed a long-established demographic trend and appears to have revived the equally long-depressed economy. Although the records are incomplete and unreliable by modern standards, we know enough about births and deaths in representative European communities in the fifteenth century to be quite certain that, with the tapering off of the calamities of famine, plague, and war which dominated the fourteenth and early fifteenth centuries, the population began to increase sharply and at an accelerating rate. We know, with equal certainty, that business improved.

In recent years, economists have tended more and more to see fluctuations in population as powerful, perhaps decisive, influences on the economic health of a society. To take the later fifteenth century as an example, it is easy to recognize that as population increased, so did the demand for grain, stimulating both a rise in prices and an expansion of production. Profits made in this, the most important, sector of the economy were either spent for imported or manufactured goods, thereby extending the stimulus from agriculture to industry and commerce, or they were invested in new production of all sorts. With prosperity, population increased still further, and with the same bewildering speed they had manifested in their common decline a century and a half before, they provided a marked, often radical, and even revolutionary stimulus to human activity.

War, Famine, and Pestilence

From 1337 to 1453, with brief respites, a confused struggle known as the Hundred Years' War had devastated France, disrupted England, and intermittently despoiled Scotland and the Low Countries. During the same general period the Iberian kings never ceased fighting among themselves except to seek conquests in Italy or to attempt to drive the Moors from their last foothold in Granada, just as the Scandinavians interrupted their civil strife only to attack the Hanseatic League. In the east, the Poles clashed with the Teutonic Knights and with Tartar raiders roving over the Ukraine, while to the south, Ottoman armies pillaged the Balkans. In addition, princes, barons, and towns fought incessantly among themselves, save on the rare occasions when they joined in a common cause to suppress revolts of the masses, who, in turn, more normally vented their frustration in frequent persecution of Jews or witches. The depredations of brigands and pirates seemed petty annoyances to a society in which victors could legitimately slaughter the vanquished they could not ransom and burn the booty they could not carry off.

Hunger still stalked Europe. Not even the drastic reduction of population during the fourteenth century had made food generally plentiful. For one thing, frequent natural calamities—floods, freezes, and droughts—produced new famines, at times so severe as to reduce men to cannibalism. In addition, even local shortages caused starvation, because fear of famine, ruthlessly exploited by speculators and political adventurers, drove most communities to forbid the export of grain, and further, because the transport of significant quantities over land was all but impossible. Finally, neither individuals nor towns had the resources, even if they had the foresight, to lay away provisions for the inevitable emergencies. Many foods could not be stored at all, and those that could, like meat and fish preserved in salt, lost most of their nutritive value if they survived rats, rot, and fire.

In the wake of war and famine came disease. Although the worst epidemics of plague struck in the fourteenth century, at least ten occurred between 1400 and 1485, and minor outbreaks were recorded somewhere every year. The towns, overcrowded and vermin-infested, with primitive ideas of public health and hygiene, were more susceptible to the plague than were rural areas; and the seaports, continually exposed to infection from the rats which swarmed around their wharves, were most vulnerable of all; but even remote and isolated communities did not escape unscathed. Yet the most murderous plagues could not claim as many victims as the common illnesses, the care and treatment of which, if attempted at all, were often more dangerous than the ailments. In the century and a half between 1300 and 1450, war, famine, and disease combined to reduce Europe's population by some 30 per cent, to about fifty million.

The Agricultural Economy

Before this great decline, almost all the inhabitants of Europe had been subsistence farmers, eking out barely enough for survival. Inevitably, they supported the rural clergy and nobility (who constituted, respectively, about 0.5 per cent and 1 per cent of the population), and those few who lived near enough had to feed the people of the towns. Well over 90 per cent of Europe's meager population, however, lived not in towns but in one of four basic types of rural environment: forest, swamp, steppe, or arable land. Forests covered much the largest portion of the continent, but both swamps and steppes also accounted for huge areas, and what remained as arable land could ill support its meager, poor, hungry, and unhealthy population.

Both in the northern plain and in the steep-walled valleys of the Mediterranean, cereals, together with some dairy products and a little meat, provided the basic diet and surpluses to pay for the inescapable rents and taxes.

Farm animals supplied power as well as food and clothing, and the wretched inhabitants understandably made
as much beer, cider, or wine as local circumstances per-
mitted. Largely <u>self-sufficient by necessity</u>, farmers sup-
plemented basic products with game, fish, and fruit from
adjacent forests and swamps. For salt, which often had to
be imported, and for any small luxuries or occasional
tools offered by peddlers or nearby market towns, they
bartered or sold their surplus.

After the onset of plagues in the fourteenth century,
population declined faster than harvests, with the result
that markets shrank and prices fell. Marginal lands were
driven out of production, and agriculture remained
depressed throughout the first half of the fifteenth century. The general shortage of labor, however, caused
wage levels in town as well as country to be maintained,
and prices of handmade goods even tended to rise. The
principal consumers of such goods were the nobles, still
predominantly landowners, whose income was suffering
a steady drop.

A significant change in the pattern of landowning followed, as a steadily increasing number of these aristocratic victims of circumstances were driven to contract
mortgages they would be unable to carry while the
depression of cereal prices continued. The ultimate result
was the <u>transfer of more and more land to thrifty peasants, who worked it themselves, thus avoiding labor costs,
or to prosperous burghers, who were eager to invest their
new wealth and who, by stricter economy and bette</u>r
<u>management, made the land yield greater returns</u> than it
did for their aristocratic predecessors. The loss of patrimony lands by prodigal nobles was greater in France,
Italy, and western Germany than in England, Spain, and

eastern Europe. Everywhere all classes hungrily eyed the vast tracts still owned by the higher clergy, who tended, because of able, professional management, to keep their estates intact.

The Business Community

Demographic decline and agricultural depression had radically transformed the economy, hurting some segments of the community and helping others. The old industries had catered primarily to aristocratic extravagance, with the result that, as the purchasing power of the nobles dropped, so did sales. Nevertheless, the skilled laborers in the established trades used the power of their well-organized guilds to prevent any lowering of wages or the introduction of laborsaving techniques, thus precluding the possibility of cutting prices. Caught in this impasse, many shop owners were forced to dismiss workers or go bankrupt. In contrast, new industries developed to meet the growing market of rural and urban workers. Benefiting from the general rise in wages, these hitherto impoverished classes began to buy cheap handmade goods which had previously been quite beyond their reach. By far the most important commodity in this category was lightweight, inexpensive woolen cloth, which could be made by less skilled and more important—unorganized labor. Bypassing the guilds and their restrictions, entrepreneurs "put out" clothmaking to peasants who in their idle seasons or hours were glad to spin or weave in their cottages, even for low wages.

The Flemish textile centers of Ypres, Bruges, and Ghent, forced by their guilds to continue turning English fleece into old-style expensive woolens, suffered. The smaller surrounding towns and villages, however, by exploiting unorganized labor and the new cheap Spanish wool, managed to prosper. The English themselves, deprived of their traditional Flemish market, were forced to follow the trend and turn their raw wool into inexpensive cloth in their own villages, in order to compete successfully with the new Flemish clothmakers. Even Florence and the other Italian cities that had made luxury cloth for most of southern Europe were forced to follow the example of the North. To switch to making the less expensive products, they too were forced to buy Spanish wool and to find cheap labor, and thus destroy their guilds and oppress their journeymen in the process.

These readjustments were both painful and hazardous, and many individuals and communities suffered; but in general, the older and better established German and Italian towns fared better than any others. The cities of northern Germany and the southern shores of the Baltic united in a protective federation called the Hanseatic League which controlled the exchange of grain, fish, furs, and forest products from the Baltic lands for cloth, metals, salt, spices, and wine from western or southern Europe. Not until the latter part of the fifteenth century was the hold of the Hansa on Baltic trade broken by the English and the Dutch. Further south, Augsburg, Nuremberg, and Ulm, to name the most important cities, escaped the general decline by continuing their long-established trade with the great Italian communes, notably Milan, Venice, and Florence, importing both the new cloth and such traditional items as silk and spices.

At least until the end of the fifteenth century, the Italians managed to maintain their position as the most successful businessmen in Europe. If they owed their previous eminence to their location at the center of the Mediterranean, they consolidated this advantage by developing the most advanced business methods of the time. Through joint-stock companies and deposit banks, they increased their ability to raise capital, and by the development of what we call insurance they shared the enormous risks involved in commerce and reduced them to a manageable factor in their accounts. The introduction of the abacus and Arabic numerals made double-entry bookkeeping possible and effective accounting practical, while bills of exchange, bought in one currency and payable at a later date in another, expanded credit at the same time they expedited commerce.

Inevitably, these superior techniques spread. Barcelona, as well as Genoa, established a state bank, while private Italian financiers concentrated banking operations at great financial capitals such as Florence, Antwerp, London, and Lyon. The Italians also established resident agents, or factors, in other principal commercial centers, and the Medici, operating from Florence, developed a close-knit and resilient business organization. A precocious forerunner of the modern holding company, this system of intricate interlocking partnerships made it possible for a branch to go bankrupt without pulling down the parent company—a possibility that would not have been comprehensible or acceptable to mediaeval businessmen. These innovations, along with many others, including the practice of investing growing profits in the governments of rising princes, clerics, and kings, began to attract imitators, notably the greatest French financier of the century, Jacques Coeur, and the rising banking family of the Fuggers in southern Germany.

Population Growth and Economic Prosperity after 1450

Between 1450 and 1500 the number of inhabitants of Europe rose from some 50,000,000 to an estimated

70,000,000, more than compensating for the demographic losses suffered since 1300. By the end of the century, the British Isles may have had 4,500,000 inhabitants; France, 15,000,000; Spain, 7,000,000; Italy, 10,000,000; Germany and the Netherlands, 10,000,000; Poland-Lithuania, 6,000,000; Greater Hungary, 3,500,000; Bohemia, 2,000,000; Russia, 6,000,000; the Balkans, 4,000,000; and Scandinavia, 2,000,000. Although the large majority of the population still lived on the land, cities began growing rapidly. Paris is estimated to have had between 100,000 and 200,000 inhabitants by the end of the century. Italy had more large towns than any other country: Milan, Venice, and Naples, each with perhaps 100,000, and several others with over 50,000. Only four cities of the Iberian Peninsula and four in the Low Countries had over 30,000. Cologne, with perhaps 40,000 persons, was the largest city in Germany; and London, with a like number, was the only city in England to exceed 15,000. Eastern Europe was far less urbanized and, except for Prague, Novgorod, Moscow, and Constantinople, probably had no towns with a population of more than 15,000. Maximum growth occurred in the eastern plains and along the western seaboard, areas which would soon provide a surplus population that would migrate across the Atlantic and the Urals. In some areas of central Europe, however, where the losses suffered in the preceding 150 years were not made up, the population remained dispersed.

Everywhere the economy responded to the stimulus of the dramatic population growth. The need for more food, housing, and clothing drove commodity prices up, and the demand for arable land outpaced the rate at which it could be cleared. Consequently, land rents and values soared, and the colonization of the less developed areas of eastern Europe, particularly in Poland and Russia, accelerated. Increased demand spurred the introduction of improved techniques, especially of crop rotation, and the quality as well as quantity of the crops improved.

But because the population grew more rapidly than new farm land could be opened and thus caused a labor surplus in the predominantly agrarian society, real wages began to fall, first on farms and later in towns as well. The consequent decline in per capita spending by both town and country laborers was, however, more than offset by the increase in their total number, which was great enough to absorb all available output. As a result, propritors enjoyed both cheaper labor costs and an expanding market for their produce. As grain prices rose, landowners prospered and, in turn, contributed to the expansion of commerce and industry by buying manufactured goods and imported luxuries. In response to this stimulus of an expanding market, industry augmented its capacity, particularly by further developing the "putting out" system. Originally designed to circumvent the guilds in a period of shrinking markets, this technique now served a different purpose in a rapidly expanding economy by drawing on the unlimited reserve of peasant labor.

This normal economic revival, however, was soon to be overtaken by a revolution in Europe's commerce. Italian capitalists, technicians, and adventurers, of whom Columbus and Amerigo Vespucci are the most famous, contributed significantly to the development of ocean trade; but even before the great discoveries, traffic along the Atlantic coastal route from the Mediterranean to the Baltic had reached an important level of activity and profit. And industry, which had hitherto been severely restricted by the limitations of mediaeval transportation, was suddenly drawn into a maelstrom of expansion.

Gradual improvements in communications had already served to expand trade. The opening of new Alpine passes between Germany and Italy shortened the routes from Italy to northern Europe, making it possible for a courier to travel overland between Venice and Bruges in a week. Useful as this speed was to expedite important negotiations, heavy or bulky goods could still be economically transported only by water, and a cargo still took three months to traverse the distance between those cities by sailing ship. Progress in techniques of water transportation had, however, continued even during the depression. Map-making, navigation, and shipbuilding all improved, so that trade between Italy and Flanders, which during the Middle Ages had used the north-south rivers, notably the Rhine, now was increasingly by sea. Sailing around Gibraltar, merchants visited the Atlantic ports en route, contributing to their development even before the advent of the transatlantic trade.

In fact, one of the most important steps in the expansion of later mediaeval commerce had been achieved by the famous "Venetian galleys." Even though there had always been some coastal shipping along Europe's Atlantic shores, no regular through trade from the Mediterranean to the North Sea and the Baltic, by way of the Atlantic, existed before the thirteenth century. About 1300, however, both the volume of commerce and nautical techniques attained levels that made such a route not merely feasible but extremely promising. Although very costly to organize, water transport, because of the enormous volume it could handle, could produce unheard-of profits. With this prospect clearly in mind, the Venetian merchants—working through their oligarchy—proceeded to solve the problems of risk owing to weather and piracy by arranging convoys of their largest galleys (propelled

by as many as 180 oars) to make the voyage to England
and the Low Countries—usually once a year. Although
precise figures are elusive, there can be no doubt that this
innovation raised the volume of north-south trade to an
entirely new order of magnitude, thereby stimulating
both manufacturing and banking to a corresponding
degree, and inevitably inviting imitators and initiating a
whole new phase of economic history.

Profits from this sea-borne commerce became too large
to be consumed in any traditional manner, so a new problem of finding opportunities for investment began to arise.
Initially this led to a further expansion and extension of
trade and then to the development of new business techniques. The results could soon be seen in the widespread
introduction of a variety of innovations. Itinerant peddlers who had supplied dispersed and limited markets by
instinct either transformed themselves, or were replaced
by, professional merchants who worked in "offices" studying reports and accounts. Large-scale speculation in
grain, wines, wool, and metals accompanied increased
investments and improved techniques. In mining, printing, spinning, and weaving, the commitment of capital
made possible the enlargement of plants and the introduction of specialization and systematic management. Under
these conditions, credit insurance and banking operations
expanded rapidly, and international business ties multiplied, building a common European economy. The new
sophisticated process of investing large sums at calculated
risks but with professional skill, in pursuit of even greater
profits, was to play an increasingly important role in
European affairs, until it dominated the entire civilization
under the name "capitalism."

Governments of the period became acutely conscious

of the unprecedented expansion of business and often sought to tap its profits. The mining industry offered an irresistible opportunity and consequently provided a fine example of this procedure. In constant and mounting need of bullion for coins and iron for arms, rulers everywhere not only maintained their traditional rights in mineral deposits but began to take an active part in the management of mines and even invested heavily in their development. Under such favorable conditions, the production of silver, lead, tin, and iron probably quintupled in central Europe between 1450 and 1530. In Italy the popes and the Medici divided the profits from vast new alum mines, while in Germany and Hungary the Hapsburgs ultimately shared the growing mining wealth with their principal bankers, the Fuggers. Simultaneously, the Portuguese began to import significant amounts of gold from western Africa. This new bullion induced a mild inflation, stimulated business, enhanced incomes, and increased the demand for all sorts of goods and services.

Rulers, encouraged by this success, attempted to extend their control to other businesses as well. Louis XI of France, for example, succeeded in establishing a fair at Lyon which lured much business away from Geneva, but he failed in his efforts to establish a native silk industry in France. In a remarkable anticipation of the mercantilism of Jean-Baptiste Colbert, his bureaucrats and theorists consciously tried to manipulate trade to build up their country's monetary reserves through the maintanance of a favorable balance of payments. Preoccupation with constantly growing needs for bullion drove kings to take increasing interest in new sources of gold and silver, particularly by encouraging the explorations which led eventually to the importation of vast American treasures.

Social Changes

The impact of these economic developments on the social structure of western Europe was profound. They deepened the political and cultural chasm dividing the increasingly commercial West from the agrarian East and wrought basic changes in both. In the West, during the depression, feudal nobles and manorial serfs had declined in number and importance as new classes arose. Until the expansion began, about 1450, aristocratic land-lords were forced to sell their grain for less and less while they had to pay more and more for labor that had once been owed them as service. The alternative was to let their lands to peasants for low rents, but the result in either case was a drastic reduction of income. Similarly, the continuous debasement and devaluation of currencies eroded revenues based on long-term leases or customary dues. Some landowners, particularly in England and Spain, protected themselves by evicting the tenants and converting their estates to sheep farms, early anticipating the enclosure movement. Others attempted to supplement their dwindling incomes by becoming professional sol-diers, bureaucrats, brigands, or—in England and Italy—even businessmen. Still others, especially in France, Spain, and the Rhineland, sank into chronic poverty, becoming the *hobereaux*, hidalgos, and *Raubritter* of the sixteenth century. Thus the shrinkage of demand for grain and the rise in labor costs before 1450 put a steady economic pressure on the noble landowners in western Europe and weakened, or at least threatened, their tradi-tional position. Most were too impoverished to benefit significantly from the expansion when it finally began.

In contrast, the serfs and agricultural laborers who survived the Black Death found their services in greatly increased demand. Landowners were forced to compete for labor with businessmen who could offer not only higher wages, but even the prospect of freedom, to escaped serfs. In certain districts, such as the English Midlands and the Castilian plateau, the early enclosure movements reduced serfs to landless rural workers and beggars, but such exceptions notwithstanding, the general scarcity of labor placed most serfs in a strong position. Frequently able to buy emancipation, to commute service obligations into money payments, or to acquire more favorable leases and even buy land, not a few during these decades ascended the social ladder from poor serf, to free peasant, to prosperous yeoman. After 1450, when their numbers began to increase rapidly, the peasants of the West, where serfdom had virtually disappeared, mitigated the effects of the decline in wages by migrating in increasing numbers to the expanding towns. In the rural East, however, having nowhere to go, the peasants were completely vulnerable to the local nobles, who proceeded to exploit them at will, ultimately reducing them to serfdom.

After a generation or two, country yeomen in the West became hardly distinguishable from urban businessmen who, upon retirement, had invested their money in farms. Sometimes both amalgamated with the poorer aristocrats in a new rural middle class which, exploiting recently acquired lands, tended to buy from and sell to townsmen, and, like the capitalists in the towns, was primarily concerned with making profits.

Turmoil and violence accompanied the rise and fall of classes in town and country. Serfs struggled for emancipation, peasants for land, and urban workers for better wages and political rights. The worst outbreaks came from the least skilled and lowest paid laborers, especially the weavers and fullers, who were ruthlessly crushed by the privileged classes. None of these popular revolts brought permanent amelioration; they only filled town and countryside with violence and arson, leaving chaos in their wake.

Following an old Judaeo-Christian tradition, the alienated, frustrated masses sought expression of, or relief from, their social discontent in religious movements promising the millennium—the establishment of an earthly kingdom of God. In the crowded cities, however, the church proved unable to alleviate the miseries of poverty or even to provide a sufficient religious opiate. The friars, who attempted to sublimate class hatred and despair, could not minister to all the rootless and desperate urban poor, while secular priests, who all too often lacked true religious commitment, were frequently not even assigned to slums. Discontent among the ignorant continued, therefore, to express itself in heresy and revolt. The overcrowded and underemployed proletariat of Prague, for example, joined the extreme wing of the Hussite movement at the beginning of the fifteenth century, and the downtrodden peasants of the region followed suit. Similarly, in Germany some of the poor mingled heresy with rebellion. Peasants' revolts multiplied in the fifteenth and early sixteenth centuries, culminating in the German Peasants' War of 1525. But these chiliastic movements failed, as thoroughly as their purely secular counterparts had, to impede the newly developing class structure of Europe.

Summary

In the West, the principal beneficiaries of the economic expansion of the latter part of the fifteenth century were the bourgeois. Because of rising prices and increasing demand, they could expect to make a profit on anything they bought and held. Agricultural producers—the peasants or yeomen in the West and the nobles in the East—also benefited from the same factors. Other classes suffered. The old feudal nobles of the West, most of whom had transmuted their manorial services or rented out their land on long-term leases, were caught with relatively fixed incomes in a period of general inflation. Even wages did not rise as fast as prices, and the proletariat, whether in town or country, was also caught at a desperate disadvantage. But while the nobles in the West lost power to the bourgeois, who now employed many of the surplus workers, those in the East succeeded in enserfing their peasants and consolidating their control of the land, thus reinforcing their social and economic dominance.

The western capitalists, with their drive for profits, began to undermine the cultural, religious, and political structures of the old agrarian world. But by their more than princely patronage, combined with their improving taste, they began to establish new ones, notably during the northern and southern Renaissances. By their new attitudes toward work and poverty, as well as by their new mental habits, they influenced the Protestant and Catholic Reformations. And finally, through heavy capital investment and the infusion of their new business methods, they aided the growth of centralized states. In eastern Europe, where few cities arose and the economy changed little, the traditional cultural, religious, and political structures tended to survive unchanged, unless —as in the case of serfdom—they were actually reinforced and extended.

Thus, although the transition from mediaeval to modern society remained incomplete, important progress in this direction had occurred by the end of the fifteenth century. The beginnings of the commercial and capitalist revolutions on the one hand, and the concomitant growth of the urban middle classes on the other, produced not merely radical economic and social changes but striking advances in the five-hundred-year-old process of territorial consolidation which constitutes the central theme of the political history of the Middle Ages. As with all important widespread developments, however, its impact was different in different parts of Europe, so that existing regional differences were often accentuated.

To follow these changes in a systematic manner it is useful to think of the map of fifteenth-century Europe as divided into four vertical strips. Along the western edge lay the national states of England, France, and Spain, which benefited most directly and most extensively from the expansion overseas. Next, between lines formed roughly by the Scheldt, Meuse, and Rhone rivers on the west and by an imaginary extension of the Elbe to the Adriatic on the east, was what we shall call west-central Europe. Here were to be found the small city-, church-, and princely states that characterized the Italian peninsula, Germany, and the Low Countries, and the old centers of commerce along the rivers that linked the Mediterranean and the North Sea. East-central Europe, between the Elbe-Adriatic line and the Dvina and Dnieper, was made up of the large, loosely organized kingdoms of Poland-Lithuania, Bohemia, and Hungary. There towns and commerce always lagged, partly because of a lack of seacoasts. Still further to the east sprawled the huge and heterogenous Muscovite and Ottoman empires tied more to the caravan trade of the Asiatic steppes than to the water-borne commerce of Europe. Just as <u>each</u> of these four strips <u>developed a characteristic economic structure,</u> and so also, by the end of the fifteenth century, each had acquired <u>distinctive regional political patterns</u>. Beginning at the center of Europe and moving first to the west and then to the east, we shall examine each of these areas as we follow the historical process of consolidation.

CHAPTER II

Principalities and City-States

THE line of the Scheldt, Meuse, and Rhone rivers separating western from west-central Europe was roughly the same as that established in 870 to divide the northern domains of Charlemagne between his surviving grandsons, Louis the German and Charles the Bald. (See, in this series, Richard E. Sullivan, *Heirs of the Roman Empire*.) This boundary remained relatively stable until early modern times, and, indeed, sections of it still constitute the long-contested Franco-German border. In the fifteenth century this line marked more than the political differences between the monarchies to the west and the city-states and principalities to the east, in central Europe. It also effectively separated the large agrarian areas in which the western monarchies were grounded from the more densely populated river valleys of Germany, the Low Countries, and northern Italy. In the latter areas the long, mutually destructive struggle between the Holy Roman Empire and the papacy had allowed the flourishing commercial and industrial towns of the Po, Rhine, and Elbe valleys and the Baltic shores to win and maintain a large degree of independence.

Grown vigorous on the trade that crossed the Alps and filtered down the rivers to the north, they were able to remain free (in fact, sovereign) or to offer sufficient resistance to both pope and emperor to preserve at least a precarious autonomy. Most, however, fell one after the other to local princes or upstarts, who, rising among the ruins of Empire and papacy, amalgamated these old independent cities into small and closely administered territorial states. The history of one city does not closely resemble that of another, but in historical perspective certain similarities appear that suggest common trends or patterns of development.

Italy

At the end of the thirteenth century, Italy emerged from its long struggle with popes and emperors to become the promised land of princes. Ostensibly the prosperous northern communes continued their famous experiments in republican government, but under the economic and social strains of the next hundred and fifty years, their constitutions became so corrupted that, sooner or later, they were subverted or suppressed by despots. Whether these new tyrants started as noblemen, regular citizens, or professional soldiers or whether they achieved power legally or seized power by force, they employed similar methods in their ascent: intricate marriage alliances, clever betrayals, and carefully plotted assassinations. Furthermore, once entrenched in power, they all had the same objectives: the establishment of hereditary ruling houses, the conquest of weaker neighbors, and the consolidation of administrative institutions. In the process of attaining their goals, they created the modern state, replete with armies, bureaucrats, and diplomatic corps.

Just after 1400, five territorial states rose from the welter of precariously independent cities to dominate the Italian peninsula. Under her great dukes, Milan became the Renaissance despotism par excellence, while Venice, despite her doge, remained an oligarchical republic. Without benefit of title, the Medici ruled Florence by dominating its rough urban politics, and the canonically elected popes attempted to govern the Papal States as absolute monarchs. Naples alone remained apparently unchanged, but even its feudal kingdom underwent significant administrative reform. Although originally jealous and suspicious of one another, these five powers soon agreed—in the Peace of Lodi (1454)—to live and let live. This treaty, which served as a putative constitution for the peninsula, not only ensured, incidentally, the survival of some of Italy's lesser states, but also instituted the first modern system of permanent resident ambassadors to oversee the peace and spy on rivals. By 1500, when as a result of the great discoveries trade and wealth were beginning to shift from the Mediterranean to the Atlantic, French and Spanish invasions precipitated the political decline of Italy and the waning of its cultural renaissance.

Milan

Milan, which dominated the western valley of the Po, had long constituted a natural center for the political, military, and commercial activity of the surrounding territories, but to subjugate and unify these turbulent dominions required the rapacious determination of a major Renaissance despot. Gian Galeazzo Visconti (1385–1402), who inherited half of Milan from his father, seized the rest by killing his uncle and succeeded in turning the old commercial and industrial commune into a modern territorial state. To gain appropriate status, he bought the title Duke of Milan from the Holy Roman Emperor and then married a French princess, with the immediate purpose of recovering respectability but with the ultimate result of providing the pretext for a French invasion of his ill-won duchy. Early resolved to expand his holdings into a kingdom in northern Italy, he was able, at his death in 1402, to bequeath to his son, Filippo Maria, a well-established principality together with the purchased title. The father's success, however, provoked retributive aggression by Venice and Florence; and the son had to spend his life in endless struggles to hold his legacy. When the male line of the Visconti came to an end with Filippo's death in 1447, a vicious struggle for the succession began.

The victor, <u>Francesco Sforza</u>, was the epitome of a particularly ruthless type of professional soldier, known in fifteenth-century Italy as <u>*condottiere.*</u> After marrying Filippo's illegitimate daughter, Sforza used his formidable military power to seize the throne of the duchy. Then, having consolidated his control of Milan, he was able, through his alliance with Florence and Naples in the Peace of Lodi, to help reduce the chronic chaos of the peninsula. Finally, by introducing irrigation, as well as the cultivation of rice and silk worms to his domains, he <u>reoriented Milan's economy toward the exploitation of the land instead of the traditional transalpine trade</u> and thus <u>fostered a new prosperity</u>. This increased wealth enabled Sforza not only to strengthen his government and army but also to patronize artists and writers, thus transforming Milan into a brilliant capital.

His son and successor, the cruel, licentious Galeazzo

Maria, left a different record. After ten years of scandalous misrule he was assassinated, to be succeeded by his
brother, Ludovico, called *il Moro*, who, as regent for
Galeazzo's eight-year-old son and heir, ruled as virtual
dictator. Even though he made Milan one of the richest
and most brilliant centers of the Renaissance, he sowed
the seeds of ultimate disaster. Seeking revenge against
Florence and Naples for disintegrating the long-standing
alliance and leaving Milan isolated, *il Moro* succeeded
in persuading the French king, Charles VIII, to come to
Italy at the head of an army to press old claims to the
kingdom of Naples. An unforeseen deviation in the
French royal succession, however, turned this maneuver
against its author.

At the time, it did not occur to Ludovico that Charles
would die without a direct heir, leaving the crown to his
cousin Louis of Orléans, who had already inherited
claims to Milan as well as Naples. When Charles died, the
victim of an accident, shortly after his Italian expedition,
Louis XII (1498–1515) mounted the throne and promptly
set out for Milan. The fact that Ludovico himself was
driven from his duchy by the invaders, who in turn were
soon replaced by the Hapsburgs as the principal foreign
overlords in Italy, made little practical difference to the
inhabitants of the city.

Venice

If this transformation of Milan from a mediaeval trading commune into a modern territorial state ruled by a
tyrant made her typical of northern Italian cities of the
fifteenth century, Venice remained unique. Secure behind
her lagoons, she continued her prosperous trade. Unaf-
fected by the confusions that wracked the rest of the

peninsula throughout the fifteenth century, the citizens of the republic had to contend with little interference, except from the dictatorial government of the city's exclusive and jealous merchant oligarchy. This rich patriciate had long promoted its economic interests by building an empire of fortified ports along the coasts and on the islands of the Adriatic and the eastern Mediterranean that discouraged or repelled foreign attack. At home factional strife was stifled by a combination of prosperity and unremitting police surveillance. The government, composed of an elected doge, or duke, a senate, and a grand council, was designed to protect the state from seizure by either a dynastic despot or a proletarian demagogue as well as from external foes.

At the beginning of the fifteenth century, Venice was actually one of the leading states of Europe. Having defeated her chief commercial rival, Genoa, she dominated the silk and spice trade of the eastern Mediterranean; and as long as she resisted the temptation to seek conquests on the mainland, she was able to avoid most of the debilitating warfare that had long engulfed the rest of Italy. Eventually, however, the consolidation of the new states in the north, particularly Milan, appeared to threaten her security. After long debate, the Venetian oligarchs reluctantly reversed their traditional policy and set out to acquire territories that would establish a protective zone to the northwest of the city. Gradually they annexed the eastern half of the Po Valley, securing their western boundary with Milan at the Adda River but at the price of being drawn into the unstable politics and sporadic wars of the peninsula. With her resources thus strained by the expense of becoming a territorial state, Venice began to lose some of her pre-eminence in the

eastern Mediterranean, where her irreconcilable conflict
with the Ottomans and mounting competition from the
Portuguese and eventually the Dutch led to her decline
in the sixteenth and seventeenth centuries.

Florence

Florence, an old commercial-industrial commune like
Milan, rounded out its possessions in Tuscany by annexing the important port of Pisa in 1406. Long governed by
a small oligarchy of rich merchants, the masters of the
seven largest guilds, or *arti maggiori*, it had, by the beginning of the fifteenth century, become the political property of an even smaller faction, headed by the Albizzi
family. Exploiting an extremely complex constitution
which appeared to guarantee equitable representation to
all classes, these patricians managed to gain effective control of the signory, or municipal administration.

In the course of the fifteenth century, however, the hold
of the Albizzi faction was broken in its turn, and a new
family, the Medici, gained control. Rising generation by
generation from obscure origins to wealth, power, and
finally nobility, the Medici personified the virtuosity and
achievement associated with the Renaissance. The foundations of family power had been laid by Giovanni di
Bicci de' Medici (1360-1429), who not only amassed an
immense fortune in commerce and banking, but associated himself with the lesser guilds and proletariat in their
resistance to the oppressive taxation of the Albizzi. His
son Cosimo, a consummate businessman, left a brilliant
career in trade and banking for politics. With the support
of the lower orders of society, he forced the Albizzi into
exile in 1434 and proceeded to rule Florence through a
balia, or reform commission with unlimited power. By
engineering an alliance with Naples and Milan to rein-

force the Peace of Lodi, he contributed not only to the pacification of Italy but to the prosperity of Florence. With an earnest love of beauty and a deep reverence for learning, he was a great patron of the arts (and artists) of his day. In addition, he was a student of the classics and an important collector of ancient manuscripts. In 1464, at the age of seventy-five, he died while listening to a reading of one of Plato's dialogues. He was succeeded first by his son Piero, then in 1469 by his grandson Lorenzo.

Lorenzo maintained both the façade of republican institutions and the practice of benevolent despotism which had characterized his grandfather's rule. He also continued to manipulate the alliance with Milan and Naples to preserve peace on the peninsula. If he was a lesser businessman than his grandfather, Lorenzo was an even more enthusiastic supporter of arts and letters. Known as "the Magnificent," this versatile intellectual became not only the Renaissance patron par excellence, but the friend of the artists, writers, and philosophers he aided. He also composed poetry which, by its intrinsic merits, has rightly earned him a high place in Italian literature. Perhaps the greatest among his many contributions to the culture of his age was his leading role in re-establishing the vernacular Italian—his own Tuscan dialect—as an acceptable vehicle for serious expression.

After Lorenzo's death in 1492, the Medici fortunes wanted. His son Piero, in a desperate effort to save Florence from Charles VIII's invading armies, surrendered a number of outlying towns to the French. Disappointed and angered by such weakness, the Florentines expelled him and attempted to revive the republic. Too long unaccustomed to self-government, however, they allowed the fanatical Savonarola to seize power. This notoriously morbid Dominican employed his demagogic

powers to overwhelm his fellow citizens with remorse for
their immorality and to convince them that their misfor-
tunes were nothing less than divine retribution. True
piety, he warned, required them to renounce the luxuries
and destroy the splendid creations of the Renaissance as
worldly "vanities." Terrified by their new-found guilt,
the populace pillaged the city for works of art, books, and
rich costumes to sacrifice in public fires and then threw
open the gates to the invading French as emissaries of
God's wrath.

Florence's neighbors, unswayed by Savonarola's pro-
phetic exhortations, kept their minds on their own mundane survival, until they suceeded first in driving the
French from the peninsula, and then in punishing
Florence for what they considered treacherous aid to the
common foe. This retribution broke the spell in which
the fanatical monk held the people of Florence, and since
his religious excesses had seriously alienated many churchmen, including the Pope, he was seized and condemned
as both a traitor and a heretic. But his public execution—he
was hanged and his body burned—did little to restore
either the reputation or unity of the republic. Florence
appeared an easy prey for any unemployed despot; yet
surprisingly, the discredited regime survived until 1512,
when the Medici returned and re-established their control.
Twenty years later, by imperial decree, they became
hereditary dukes and, as such, ruled until 1737. This "first
family" of Florence, it should be noted, produced several
cardinals, three popes, and two queens of France.

The Papacy and the Church

By the fifteenth century, the papacy, too, was creating
a territorial state. The very gravity of the problems which
threatened the later mediaeval church—schism, concili-

arism, heresy, and Islam—seemed to force the popes to rely more and more on their own princely resources in the Patrimony. After their narrow escape from the ultimate threat of subjection to conciliar authority, however, the Renaissance popes became increasingly preoccupied with humanism and art or simply with their own personal fortunes, to the detriment not only of the church but of the Papal States as well. Still, badly as they managed the church, these successors of St. Peter were able, thanks to the revenues they wrung from Christendom, particularly Germany, to subjugate the various local powers in the vicinity of Rome.

Having been absent in Avignon during much of the fourteenth century and then weakened by the schism, the popes had long since lost effective control of the Papal States. In 1414, after a period of almost fifty years during which there were first two, and finally three, claimants to the title (see, in this series, Robert E. Lerner, *The Age of Adversity: The Fourteenth Century*), cardinals from the various rival camps finally succeeded in convening one of the largest and most important councils ever held. Meeting at Constance, it began by deposing all three pretenders to St. Peter's throne and then, in 1417, elected Martin V, thus reuniting western Christendom under a single pope. Martin's successor had to beat down attempts by subsequent councils to assume control of the church and was himself forced to squander a large part of his resources fighting against the followers of the heresiarch John Hus, who had been burned by the Council of Constance.

Significantly, Nicholas V (1447–1455), the first postconciliar pope, concentrated his energies on re-establishing his position in Rome and refurbishing his Vatican Palace. Employing humanists to collect, copy, and edit the classical manuscripts that still form the nucleus of the Vatican Library, and enlisting countless artists and architects, he supervised the restoration of the Eternal City as the seat of Christendom. The fall of Constantinople in 1453 cast a shadow on Nicholas' achievements, as well as on the papacy; and one of his great humanist successors, Pius II (1458–1464), spent much of his pontificate in a vain attempt to launch a crusade to free that city from the Turks.

But later, more cynical popes concentrated their efforts more openly and ruthlessly on achieving success in Italian politics. When the Spaniard Rodrigo Borgia, nephew of a previous pontiff, mounted the papal throne as Alexander VI (1492–1503), the Renaissance papacy reached a kind of apogee. Demonstrating that he recognized no conflict between his papal duties and his personal ambitions, Alexander established for all posterity a record for urbane clerical corruption. To capture the papacy, he put aside his common-law wife and, according to contemporary rumor, bought the tiara with his personal fortune. To extend his new power he directed his daughter, Lucrezia, through a series of marriages with Italian despots and used every opportunity that the papacy afforded to secure place and power for his family.

Determined to reconquer the subject cities that had been seized by local despots during the Avignonese captivity and the schism, Alexander put his son, Cesare Borgia, in command of the papal armies. Refined, elegant, and charming, though utterly unscrupulous, Cesare proved to be an excellent commander and an able administrator. In three major campaigns he restored practically all the lost territory, thus re-establishing the Pope's political authority over the Papal States. As a result, both

Cesare and Alexander appeared to personify what the Renaissance called _virtù, daring and ruthless cleverness resulting in worldly success._ But this triumph of political tyranny and fiscal extortion, just like the earlier victory over the councils, had been _won at the cost of spiritual leadership. Corruption flourished unheeded and unchecked_ throughout the western church.

Naples

In contrast to the city-states of the north, Naples was a _feudal monarchy based on an agricultural economy._ Geographically accessible to conquest, it had long suffered under foreign misrule; and when a century and a half of stagnation under the French house of Anjou came to a catastrophic climax in the scandalous reign of the degenerate Joanna II, even reform came from abroad. Upon the mad queen's death in 1435, Alfonso the Magnanimous of Aragon drove out the Angevin claimant to the throne and added Naples to his Spanish and Sicilian holdings. Alfonso (d. 1458) and his bastard son, Ferrante I, strove to impose a centralized administration on the feudal structure of southern Italy. They suppressed the surviving Angevin supporters, reorganized state finances, and encouraged the investment of foreign, largely Florentine, capital. Both men, but especially Alfonso, were notable patrons of art, letters, and scholarship who sought to make their court a show place of Renaissance culture. After the Peace of Lodi, Alfonso helped construct the alliance of Naples, Florence, and Milan; but by supporting a papal attempt to break the power of the Medici, Ferrante lost the confidence of his allies. There is little doubt, however, that he and his father were the outstanding Neapolitan rulers of the fifteenth century. It was the

death of Ferrante that prompted his old enemies at home
and abroad—Angevin sympathizers, the Pope, and the
Milanese under the leadership of Ludovico Sforzo—to
urge Charles VIII of France to press his claims to the
crown of Naples. The consequent French invasion of
1494 and the Spanish counterattack it provoked ravaged
southern Italy, leaving it under uninterrupted foreign
occupation that turned it into one of the most backward
regions of Europe.

Germany

In Germany, as in Italy, the fifteenth century was the
period of the prince. Since the collapse of the Empire in
the middle of the thirteenth century, despite such efforts
at reconstruction as Charles IV's Golden Bull (see
Lerner, *Age of Adversity*), Germany had gradually
slipped toward anarchy. The flourishing cities along the
trade routes managed to affirm their *de facto* independence and exerted what influence they could for the
maintenance of peace and order, but unlike their greater
counterparts in Italy, they were unable to extend their
domination to the countryside. Emperors, electors (the
seven great magnates, lay or clerical, who, according to
the terms of the Golden Bull, chose the Emperor), nobles,
townsmen, and clerics all placed their particular interests
above those of Germany as a whole. In the course of the
fifteenth century, however, this disintegrative process
was partially checked by the emergence of strong regional
rulers collectively known as princes. A score of powerful
lay and ecclesiastical lords, by consolidating medium-
sized territories, managed to subdue most of their local
rivals and eventually to achieve regional autonomy. Several founded major dynasties, which not only prospered

but survived until the ultimate collapse of the German Empire in 1918. Of these, the most powerful in 1400 was the House of Luxemburg, whose greatest possession was not its ancestral county but its recently acquired kingdom of Bohemia, the only monarchy in the Empire. Later the Hapsburgs in Swabia and Austria, the Wettins in Saxony, the Wittelsbachs in the Palatinate and Bavaria, and finally the Hohenzollerns in Brandenburg and Prussia were to exercise great influence in German affairs. In addition, lesser princes, including the ecclesiastical electors —the archbishops of Mainz, Trier, and Cologne—succeeded in amassing incomparably greater wealth and authority than ordinary nobles.

The Princes and the Emperors

Traditionally, princes were subordinate to the emperor, but in practice they were frequently his equals. Since he had almost none of the legislative authority that might be expected to go with his exalted title, he would have needed the cooperation of the unwieldy parliament (diet) to make new laws; and to enforce them he had little but his own personal and very limited resources. The imperial office was thus hardly more than an empty dignity.

In Germany, as in the rest of Europe, the fourteenth century had closed on a scene of mounting chaos. Electors and princes had deposed the incompetent Wenceslas, to replace him on the imperial throne with the ignominious Rupert of the Palatinate (1400–1410), who climaxed an inept reign by launching an expedition to Italy, which proved so embarrassingly futile that to get back to Germany he was obliged to pawn his crown. Upon his death, the electors transferred that tarnished symbol to Sigismund (1410–1437), the younger brother of the deposed Wenceslas. Vain, profligate, and capricious, Sigismund was also charming, generous, and learned, and perhaps the most nearly illustrious emperor of the later Middle Ages. He was, however, no match for the anarchy, heresy, foreign enemies, and economic depression that plagued the Empire. (See Chapter IV.)

Although Sigismund spent his life rushing headlong from defeat to defeat, he achieved one notable success by summoning the Council of Constance. Public opinion had long favored calling an assembly to end the papal schism which had divided the western church since 1378; but none of the contending popes had ever been willing to support this solution and accept the implicit risk of being deposed. Finally, however, in 1413 the schismatic pope who called himself John XXIII, having been driven from Rome by the king of Naples, begged protection of the Emperor. Sigismund seized the occasion to force John to agree to a general council and then summoned the two other papal claimants, together with all Christian princes and prelates, to meet in the imperial city of Constance. In addition to presiding in person, the Emperor played a vigorous role in the affairs of the council, exacting submission from the rivals and guiding the assembled fathers toward common action. When the field was finally cleared of contenders and a single successor agreed on, Sigismund was the hero of the day.

In 1438 he was succeeded on the imperial throne by his son-in-law, Albert of Hapsburg. This prince, in spite of the fact that he had been looked to as a promising successor, actually achieved little beyond the acquisition of the title of Albert II, since he survived Sigismund less than a year. That act, in itself, however, sufficed to launch the Hapsburg family on an almost unbroken line of imperial succession that lasted until the abolition of the title in 1806. During a long and empty reign, Albert's cousin and successor, Frederick III (1439–1493), allowed Germany to plunge even deeper into civil strife while he devoted his meager energies to strengthening the Hapsburg position. In this pursuit he achieved his greatest and possibly least expected triumph, the marriage of his son and heir, Maximilian, to Mary, the daughter and heiress of Charles the Bold of Burgundy. Elected official heir apparent with the title King of the Romans in 1486, Maximilian took charge of the Empire before his father's death and, from the powerful base of his Austrian and Burgundian possessions, began to restore imperial prestige by military successes.

In an attempt to capitalize on his triumphs, Maximilian convoked a diet at Worms in 1495 to draft a workable constitution for the Empire. First he secured the right to collect a tax called the "common penny," then he established an imperial supreme court, and finally he persuaded the legislators to outlaw private wars and confederations within the Empire. Maximilian intended these changes to help re-create a central government; but throughout the rest of his reign, his jealous princes forced from him one concession after another, until, at his death in 1519, little of the centralized authority for which he had struggled so hard remained for his successor. In contrast, the marriage of his son, Philip, to Joanna the Mad, the daughter and eventual heiress of Ferdinand and Isabella of Spain, was to leave a major imprint on European history by binding the crumbling Empire to the fastest rising national monarchy in Europe.

Rivals to the Princes: Clergy, Knights, Towns

Even if the princes did succeed in establishing themselves as the most powerful and favored class in fifteenth-
century Germany, three other deeply entrenched groups
managed to survive as active rivals: the clergy, the free
knights, and the burghers. All three saw their positions
gradually erode, in spite of their vigorous, if ill-coordi-
nated efforts, at self-preservation. Theoretically they
could have cooperated for their common defense against
the encroachments of the princes, but too often each
group resorted to its own characteristic and individualistic devices.

Perhaps the chief obstacle to the political consolidation
of Germany, though ironically not to the ambitions of
the princely families, was the church. As a result, in part,
of the early mediaeval practice of using churchmen as
imperial administrators, almost a sixth of the country was
under the jurisdiction of clerical rulers who acted as
temporal lords. Some actually bore secular titles, but
virtually all shared the views and objectives, as well as
the rank and prestige, of their lay colleagues. The chief
difference between the two was that the clerical lords,
deprived of the possibility of legitimate heirs by their
vow of celibacy, were precluded from the normal practice
of bequeathing their offices and lands to their own off-
spring. Instead, succession was normally established by
ecclesiastical elections in which local princely families
frequently had sufficient influence to reserve bishoprics
for their own younger sons. The bishops of Strasbourg,
Speyer, and Würzburg, quite as much as the more famous
archbishop-electors of Mainz, Trier, and Cologne, were
in practice lay princes. The members of the lower clergy,

over which these worldly prelates presided, were left
largely to their own devices, with the result that they
earned a reputation for lack of discipline, mismanagement
of funds, and the perversion of offices for personal or
political gain. For obvious reasons, the secular princes
had as little interest in the reform of such a rich and
corrupt establishment as the great clerics themselves.
The consequences of this shameless abuse of clerical
incomes and prestige were to be experienced a century
later in the wholesale confiscation of ecclesiastical lands
and prerogatives during the Protestant Reformation.

Unlike the princes and upper clergy, few of the once
proud barons and knights (*Ritter*) continued to enjoy
the prestige and position accorded them during the high
Middle Ages. Although many managed to maintain a
precarious independence under the nominal authority of
the emperor, they were jealous of the prosperous
burghers, resentful of the powerful princes, and frequently in mortal conflict with both. Because as nobles
they were prohibited by pride, tradition, and in some
cases, law, from associating with burghers or engaging in
trade, they were driven increasingly to banditry as the
only occupation appropriate to their station, and even
that usually failed to mend their dilapidated fortunes.
The degrading poverty that transformed them into "rob-
ber barons" contributed to the mounting bitterness that
would eventually incite many to join Martin Luther's
revolt.

During the later Middle Ages, wealth and culture
in Germany was concentrated in the cities. Although
small by modern standards, these prosperous, resourceful
communities produced art, architecture, literature, and
scholarship of remarkable quality. Under the titular pro-

tection of the emperor, the "free imperial cities" enjoyed privileges and independence which they defended vigorously against repeated and tremendously destructive attacks by the rising princes. The greatest threat to urban survival, however, proved to be the gradual divergence to the Atlantic of the traditional north-south trade. Economically weakened by this shift, some of the cities eventually succumbed to the growing power of the princes; and all started on the gradual decline that would continue into the nineteenth century.

Estates and Leagues

Although all three of these threatened groups—the nobility, the clergy, and, to a lesser degree, the towns— were represented in regional assemblies called *Landtage*, or estates, they failed to make effective use of this mediaeval institution in their struggle with the princes. In fact, these legislative bodies which might have been expected to oppose the growing authority of the new princely bureaucracies tended to contribute to their consolidation. Since their constituents were interested primarily in peace, order, and efficient government, the deputies in the *Landtage* were as eager as the new administrators to differentiate between public finances and the ruler's private resources and to create a quasi-independent judiciary. They even attempted to impose primogeniture on the ruling families by law, in order to obstruct their ancient custom of dividing lands among all male heirs. In the long run all these efforts at reform had the effect of strengthening the position of the princes, but probably none more than the expanding use of Roman law, which the *Landtage* encouraged in their efforts to further judicial reform. Originally revived by the Italian law schools in the twelfth century for clerical and commercial use, the Roman code was gradually employed in Germany by all—princes and *Landtage* included—who were interested in reinforcing civil authority. More comprehensive and systematic than Germanic custom, the Roman code buttressed the authority of administrative government and recognized the sovereign as the source of all rights and power.

Though the *Landtage* ended by serving rather than opposing the forces of centralization, another mediaeval institution, the urban league, did pose a formidable obstacle to princely progress. The most famous was the organization of commercial cities in the north known as the Hansa (see above, Chapter I). In addition, the nobles, cities, and bishops of Swabia formed their own league to restore and maintain order in the south. The most notable of all, however, was the Helvetic, or Swiss, Confederation, which gained control of many of the crucial Alpine passes linking Italy with Germany. In existence since the end of the thirteenth century, it gained formal recognition as an independent power in 1394, thanks mainly to a spectacular series of military victories over the French, the Burgundians, and the Hapsburgs. As a result, the citizens of the Helvetic League enjoyed more freedom than any other Europeans, even though the member cantons squandered its benefits in fighting among themselves and refused to share them with the inhabitants of territories they conquered. Even if the members of the League, torn by tensions between German-, French-, and Italian-speaking regions, and by endemic factional strife, were incapable of consummating a stable federal organization, their stubborn courage, backed up by superb natural defenses and a formidable military reputation, preserved their independence and, by later providing a safe haven for Zwingli, Calvin, and their followers, proved to be an important factor in the Reformation.

Burgundy

Among the new princes, by far the most spectacular were the dukes of Burgundy. By gaining control of the commercial and industrial cities of the lower Rhine, Meuse, and Scheldt, they had succeeded in dominating the main northern terminals of the old mediaeval trade routes and thus, in less than a century, had come into possession of wealth exceeding that of any other rulers in Europe. The founder of the dynasty, Philip the Bold (1363–1404), had received the duchy of Burgundy from his father, John of France, as a royal appanage. Then, by marriage, he added the counties of Flanders, Artois, Nevers, Rethel, and the imperial Free County of Burgundy (Franche-Comté). Not content with these acquisitions, he persuaded the widowed and childless duchess of Brabant and Limburg to bequeath her holdings to one of his sons and arranged a marriage for a daughter, as well as another son, with the family ruling Holland, Zeeland, and Hainault. Philip's successor, John the Fearless (1404–1419), proved no less shrewd at the marriage game than his father, with the result that his own son, Philip the Good (1419–1467), found himself lord of the French and German Burgundies and all of the Netherlands.

The very extent of Philip's holdings robbed them of any unity. The Burgundies (the French duchy and the imperial county) were primarily agricultural and therefore poorer and less populous than the duke's other possessions in the Low Countries. All his lands, however, were inhabited by peoples of mixed Teutonic and Latin

The Burgundian possessions

extraction who spoke Germanic or French dialects, just
as each major portion lay partly within the Holy Roman
Empire (the county of Burgundy and the Low Countries)
and partly within the realm of France (Flanders and
the duchy of Burgundy). The only common bond
between these scattered and varied territories was their
duke, Philip the Good.

 That ambitious prince had three major aims: first, to
round out his territories by acquiring the strip separating
Burgundy from the Low Countries; second, to link them
permanently through a unified and centralized administration; and finally, to gain a royal crown. The first he
nearly achieved. In 1421 he purchased the county of
Namur and in 1455 had one of his sons invested with the
rich bishopric of Utrecht. A year later he secured the
election of a nephew to the still richer see of Liège, and
then purchased the extensive duchy of Luxemburg. But
when he set his sights on Lorraine, the last piece of the
territorial jigsaw puzzle, the king of France recognized
the threat and declared war.

 The administrative integration of all these territories,
however, proved more difficult than their acquisition. In
each, Philip was accepted as the right and lawful but
wholly local ruler. To the Burgundians he was their duke,
to the Flemings their count, and to the Dutch the count
of Holland. Thus, in the exercise of his sovereign rights
in each, he was bound by local laws and customs. In spite
of these restrictions, Philip and his successor, Charles the
Bold, did manage to impose some degree of centralization
on their various lands. By subordinating the temporal
power of the church to their direct control and subjecting
it to taxation, they established both an important source
of revenues and a kind of ready-made bureaucracy. The

Great Council, composed of members from all the provinces, dealt with matters of general concern and gradually extended its authority over areas not protected by well-entrenched local customs. Financial matters were centralized in the Chambre des Comptes and appellate jurisdiction for all the domains invested in a parlement at Mechlin. After 1463, delegates from all local assemblies met at Bruges in an estates-general; and from 1471, a standing army was recruited from, and supported by, all the provinces.

Having thus created a *de facto* kingdom, Duke Philip was determined to secure the appropriate title to go with it. His establishment of the Golden Fleece, the most famous and magnificent of chivalric orders, served notice of his intention. His opulent court made this "Grand Duke of the West" the envy of his fellow sovereigns, but his dream of reconstituting the ninth-century realm of Charlemagne's grandson Lothair—the middle kingdom stretching between France and Germany from the Low Countries to the Alps—terrorized them. Philip, as a result, found his insistent quest for the coveted royal title resolutely turned aside with offers of the humiliating compromise designation, "King of Brabant."

In 1467, Charles the Bold inherited his father's titles and ambitions, but as the famous chronicler Philippe de Commynes recounts, "He had neither the sense nor the malice to carry off his designs." Even so, he made impressive, if temporary, additions to the Burgundian inheritance and prestige. First he ruthlessly crushed revolts in several of his Netherlandish cities, and then he secured a *de facto* mortgage from the Hapsburgs on their holdings in Alsace. Next he annexed the duchy of Guelders, and finally he assumed the protectorate of Liège and Lorraine.

All this he clearly intended to cap with the marriage of his daughter, Mary, to Maximilian, son of Emperor Frederick III. Late in 1473, Charles and Frederick met at Trier to work out the details. Tentatively, they agreed that Mary's dowry would be the entire Burgundian inheritance; that Charles, as the defender of Christendom, would lead a crusade against the Turks; and that the emperor would create the long-desired kingdom of Burgundy, including, in addition to the existing dominions, the bishoprics of Utrecht, Liège, Toul, and Verdun, together with the duchies of Clèves, Lorraine, and Savoy. When everything seemed ready for final ratification, Maximilian suddenly and inexplicably sailed down the Moselle in the middle of the night, leaving Charles the laughingstock of Europe.

To insult was rapidly added injury. Finding himself suddenly faced with a hostile coalition of the duke of Lorraine, the Swiss cantons, and his archenemy Louis XI of France, Charles seized the initiative. After overrunning Lorraine, he rashly attacked the Swiss on their own terrain, where, at Morat in 1476, his ill-disciplined semifeudal forces were surrounded and slaughtered by the tough mountain soldiers of the cantons. Six months later Charles suffered a final disaster when, along with most of his troops, he was cut down at Nancy. So great was the carnage that Lord Byron reported seeing bones of the Burgundian dead when he visited the battlefields in 1816.

Morat and Nancy marked the beginning of the end of the Burgundian dream. To secure acceptance as her father's successor to the ducal throne, Mary had to grant a charter of <u>"Great Privilege" (1477)</u> abolishing much of the centralized administration and restoring many old regional liberties. At this point Louis XI launched an invasion to back his demand that Mary wed his son the dauphin, driving the desperate young duchess to find a protector in Maximilian of Hapsburg. Still legally his fiancée, she hastily arranged the long-delayed marriage, and Maximilian as quickly took up the defense of his new wife's realm. Having restored order in the provinces and concluded peace with France in 1482, he was able, when Mary died the same year, to have their infant son, Philip, declared her successor in all the Burgundian territories. When Maximilian became emperor in 1493, Philip, known to history as "the Handsome," took over actual administration of this inheritance. His marriage to Joanna the Mad, daughter of Ferdinand and Isabella, however, was destined to subordinate Burgundian and Netherlandish interests to those of Spain, diverting his ancestors' grandiose dreams of territorial aggrandizement to new regions. In 1500, with the death of the last male heir, Joanna became heiress presumptive to the several Spanish crowns and all their dependencies in the Old World and the New. Philip's attention was inevitably and increasingly occupied by this immense inheritance.

CHAPTER III

The Western Monarchies

WHILE princes were successfully consolidating their new city-states in Italy, Germany, and Burgundy, hereditary kings were busy welding the great fiefs of France and England and the petty kingdoms of the Iberian Peninsula into centralized monarchies. These royal governments, not having been undermined by papal intervention, as was the Holy Roman Empire (see, in this series, Sidney Painter, *The Rise of the Feudal Monarchies*), were eventually able to tighten the loose feudal bonds linking the nobles to the crown. Further, since agriculture predominated in this area west of the Scheldt, Meuse, and Rhone—at least until the trans-European trade began to be diverted from the overland routes to the Atlantic—towns were generally too weak to attempt to gain their independence. Instead, they cooperated with the emerging bureaucratic authority of the central monarchies against the anarchic misrule of the feudal nobles. With this support, and without the opposition of rich and powerful trading cities of the sort that had checked the ambitions of would-be kings in west-central Europe, the new royal governments of the West were able to subject the nobility, control the clergy, and create new fiscal administrations.

The Consolidation of States: Final Phase

Dynastic marriage-making was the favorite, if not always successful, technique of the "new monarchs" in their untiring efforts to extend their authority. Near the beginning of the century, the English king, Henry V, had attempted to acquire the French crown and end the Hundred Years' War by marrying the French Princess Catherine. Although this plan proved to be overambitious, Henry Tudor, somewhat later, was able to consolidate his hold on the English crown, which he had won in battle, by marrying Elizabeth of York, the heiress of his chief rival. And toward the end of the century Charles VIII added Brittany to the French crown by marrying the Duchess Anne. Most famous of all was the marriage of Ferdinand of Aragon and Isabella of Castile in 1469. By uniting the two most important Iberian kingdoms, it laid the foundation for a great national monarchy in Spain.

In England and France, and to a lesser extent in Spain, one of the chief obstacles to the development of monarchical authority was the stubborn resistance of the princely rulers of the great appanages. Since the thirteenth century kings had frequently granted huge estates, called appanages, to younger sons who were not expected to inherit the crown (see Painter, *Rise of the Feudal Monarchies*), and by the end of the Middle Ages the practice was bearing bitter fruit in both England and France. In fact, throughout Europe appanages had grown so enormously in both size and number that they not only challenged royal authority but even occasionally became autonomous states.

The new monarchs were diligent in their task of revamping old, and creating new, instruments of government. The kings of England, France, and Spain centered their growing bureaucracies in the royal council, which often acted as the supreme court of the realm. At the same time, new royal agents, or "king's men" as they were called, increasingly insinuated themselves into the administration of local, feudal, and ecclesiastical courts, with the result that both laws and legal procedures became more uniform and effective, and the authority of the monarchy was extended and entrenched. Finally, new standing armies composed of infantry and cavalry supported by archers (later by artillery) established their superiority in the Hundred Years' War and, because they were too expensive for any save national monarchies to maintain, greatly reinforced the new royal power. The effectiveness of these forces was further demonstrated in the capture of Granada from the Moors in 1492 and in the French invasion of Italy two years later.

The cost of the new bureaucracies and armies, however, could not be met by existing royal resources. In England, France, and Spain, the king's ordinary revenues from crown lands, feudal dues, commodity monopolies, customs duties, and mint rights had declined seriously by 1300; and the traditional income from mines, markets tolls, fines, fees, and vacant fiefs or ecclesiastical benefices dwindled to insignificance. Even the feudal taxes and church grants, upon which the new monarchs now depended, were irregular and infrequent, and to make matters worse, existing fiscal machinery was inadequate and out of date. Various expedients, such as borrowing at great discounts against future revenue or imposing forced loans, produced limited returns but no ultimate solutions. The inescapable conclusion confronting all monarchs was that taxes had to be collected more regularly and frequently. In France feudal payments such as scutages (taxes paid in lieu of customary service) and aids (money given to an overlord for unusual expenses) (see, in this series, Sidney Painter, *Mediaeval Society*) were combined with "extraordinary" taxes, theoretically levied on burghers for the defense of the realm in time of crisis, and all were collected annually. In other areas a greater reliance was placed on increased sales taxes, like the *alcabala* in Castile. In England the king failed to institute a high permanent tax but gained more control of existing revenues, especially of customs on wool and cloth. If, at the end of the century, royal income still remained inadequate for growing needs, the monarchs were, nevertheless, finally in command of sufficient resources to overwhelm any combination of recalcitrant feudal lords.

Increasingly the new centralized states either won the support of, or imposed their authority on, the more important elements of society. The church, weakened by schism, became everywhere more dependent on royal protection and more subservient to national interests. The once disputed Gallican Liberties—the doctrine that the church in France was not subject to direct papal control—was formally recognized in the Pragmatic Sanction of Bourges in 1438, thus virtually transforming French bishops into royal agents. In Spain, too, the kings dominated the church, and through it the formidable power of the Inquisition, while in England the tradition of the crown's authority in religious matters, already

established in the fourteenth century by limitations on
the rights of foreign clergy to visit England and of English clergy to appeal to foreign (i.e., papal) courts—in
the Statutes of Provisors and Praemunire—was maintained and reinforced. More important, the bourgeoisie
rallied to the monarchs, largely in return for protection
of their trade and preservation of the peace. French kings
kept close watch on town governments and finances and
made increasing use of bourgeois officials in the royal
administration. The Spanish crown exercised less direct
control of town affairs but pursued a policy of close
cooperation with the burghers; and the English kings
drew support from their commercial classes. Only the old
feudal nobility failed, as a class, to contribute to the
development of the new monarchies; but it was already
too much weakened by foreign and civil wars and by
economic changes to be of decisive importance.

While in west-central Europe common interests tended
to develop within the limited territories of new city-states
and principalities, reinforcing regionalism, the new monarchies in the West extended their jurisdiction to the
larger areas of the nation-state. Nationalism—the self-
conscious advocacy of the common cause of a "people"
defined by political and linguistic associations—has
become a dominant factor only in the nineteenth and
twentieth centuries. Even so, the awareness of speaking a
common language and obeying a single ruler gave men
of the fifteenth century the conviction that they shared
economic and political interests, especially when the
group or "nation" became personified in hero figures.

Spain

At the opening of the fifteenth century, the Iberian
Peninsula was split into the three Christian kingdoms of

Castile, Aragon, and Portugal, the Moorish kingdom of Granada, and the tiny Christian kingdom of Navarre, which crossed the Pyrenees into France. With the exception of Aragon, these Iberian states had had little contact with the rest of Europe. Not only were they isolated by strong provincial traditions, but they were also divided into smaller units by innumerable local customs and institutions. Aragon, for example, was comprised of Aragon proper, Valencia, the Balearic Islands, and Catalonia. By the beginning of the sixteenth century, however, the five Iberian kingdoms had been reduced to two. Portugal was becoming a rich commercial nation, and Spain, thanks to a vast colonial empire in the New World and important possessions in Italy, was about to emerge as Europe's greatest power.

During the early fifteenth century, the nobles, clergy, and towns of the peninsula continued to exercise their ancient privileges and rights to exemptions, largely unhampered by their weak kings. Soon, however, a strong and stable monarchy appeared in Portugal. In alliance with the prosperous trading towns of the Atlantic littoral, the crown subdued the nobles and, through the inspired leadership of Prince Henry the Navigator, placed the kingdom in the forefront of European exploration and oceanic commerce. Ironically, however, in Castile, where the king sometimes claimed the title of emperor, the crown was weaker than in any monarchy in Europe except the Holy Roman Empire. The absence of effective central government was largely due to the Islamic occupation and the long bitter struggle for the reconquest of the peninsula. The cities and towns, for example, were more often fortified centers of refuge from Moorish attack than true trading centers, and as a result had long carried the burdens and exercised the privileges of precarious, *de facto* independence. Largely on the basis of this essentially democratic military service, representatives of the towns dominated the Cortes, or representative assembly, particularly in matters involving money. In addition, the great nobles, or *ricos hombres*, tended to ignore the crown, while members of the clergy and the military orders had won, as a reward for their struggle with Islam, the privileges of tax exemption and the right of being judged by canon law. In Aragon, however, it was the towns that were weak and the nobles that controlled the Cortes. The intransigent independence of these great aristocrats is reflected in the very oath of allegiance to their king that tradition ascribes to them: "We, who are as good as you, swear to you, who are no better than we, to accept you as our king and sovereign lord, provided you observe all our liberties and laws: but if not, not." Finally, the great Catalonian port of Barcelona, because of its size and wealth a phenomenon in itself, was able to use the military resources of the Aragonese crown to serve its interests. The acquisition of Sicily in 1410 and of Naples in 1434 made Barcelona the dominant commercial power on the western Mediterranean.

The culmination of Spain's mediaeval history came with the marriage of Isabella and Ferdinand in 1469 and the consequent union of Castile and Aragon. Following a complicated and protracted controversy over the succession to the Castilian throne, this marriage aroused strong opposition. The kings of Portugal and France tried desperately to prevent it, as did many nobles and rivals of Isabella in her native Castile. In eloquent testimony to the strength of the opposition, the Aragonese Prince Ferdinand slipped into a private home in Castile, disguised as a merchant, to celebrate what the outside world and subsequent historians would regard as a particularly brilliant royal marriage.

The political result was the creation of something like a confederation. Castile and Aragon each retained its own Cortes, councils, laws, courts, armies, taxes, coins, and sovereignty. The subjects of the one were aliens in the other, and in theory there was neither a king of Spain nor a Spanish kingdom. In practice, however, the union produced important mutual advantages for both states, even though Castile rapidly became the dominant partner. Aragon, already suffering from the general stagnation of Mediterranean commerce, could still carry on her mercantile and maritime tradition by aiding the Castilians in their transatlantic ventures. Castilian wool was manufactured into cloth in, and exported by, Barcelona, a port Columbus had frequented long before he began serving Castile. In return, Castilian troops supported and even expanded Aragon's Mediterranean empire, until by 1529 it dominated all of Italy. Thus began the amalgamation of the two major Spanish kingdoms.

Their Catholic majesties, Ferdinand and Isabella, set out to replace the old mediaeval administration with a new central bureaucracy. First they reduced the great nobles to a courtier class by forcing them to disgorge huge sums to the royal treasury, by systematically demolishing their castles, and by transferring their authority in local administration to agents of the crown. Finally, with the Audiencia, a powerful secular court, the monarchs developed an effective means of dealing with recalcitrant aristocrats when normal administrative methods failed. The palace guard, created to siphon off the military energies of the nobility, became the nucleus of a royal standing army; and the hitherto independent and powerful military orders of fighting monks were brought under royal command by the expedient of forcing each order to elect King Ferdinand Grand Master. The old *hermandades*, leagues of towns with their own armed forces, were reorganized as a royal police to maintain law and order. Central control of local affairs was further reinforced by the appointment of royal watchdogs, or *corregidors*, within the towns, which now benefiting more from the unaccustomed order than they ever had from their old liberties, raised no serious objections to the practice. This new central power was exercised through a maze of mediaeval councils that was gradually enlarged, restaffed, and wholly transformed into a dedicated and independent royal bureaucracy, supported by the Cortes' imposition of permanent new taxes such as the *alcabala*. The church, too, was reduced to subservience and reorganized. The famous Inquisition, for example, which was originally established in Castile to deal with Jews and Moors suspected of mere token conversion to Christianity and which came to epitomize the union of political and religious power, directed its energies as much to support the interests of the crown as to punish covert dissenters from the faith. The disenfranchisement of Jews and their eventual expulsion in 1492 were undertaken quite as much to bring vast quantities of confiscated wealth to the royal treasury as to purge the religious community.

At the end of the century the consolidated Spanish monarchy rounded out its territories by new conquests and capped its successes with world-wide explorations. In 1492 the capitulation of the kingdom of Granada to the Catholic monarchs finally completed, after nearly eight hundred years, the reconquest of the peninsula from the Moslems. Although the subjugated Moslems were to suffer a fate similar to that of the Jews, the first victims of this victory were Ferdinand's Christian neighbors. By 1512 he had occupied and annexed the portion of the kingdom of Navarre south of the Pyrenees, thus bringing all of the peninsula, except Portugal, under his sway.

While waiting for the fall of Granada in 1491, however, their Catholic majesties were approached by a Genoese ship captain with a plan for sailing across the Atlantic to the Orient. Apparently attracted by the personality of Christopher Columbus, and certainly jealous of the Portuguese and their African route to the East, Isabella backed an expedition that set sail August 3, 1492, under the aegis of Castile. On March 15, 1493, Columbus returned triumphant to announce a golden age for Spain and, although he did not know it, to give her the keys to a fabulous new world.

France

Bled by half a hundred years of war, France, at the opening of the fifteenth century, was being drained of her last remaining energies by a scandalous court and a notoriously corrupt administration. The king, Charles VI (1380–1422), was mad; and his brother, the duke of Orléans, as well as his uncles the dukes of Burgundy and Berry and his cousin the duke of Anjou, all vied for his power and wealth. The treacherous assassination of the duke of Orléans by his cousin the duke of Burgundy plunged the country into civil war just as it faced a new onslaught by the young and dashing Henry V of England, who hoped to make good his claims to the crown of France.

Crossing the channel in 1415, Henry V met the French

at Agincourt. The English forces were few but formidable, and the French nobles, remembering nothing from the debacles of Crécy or Poitiers, constituted an anachronistic mediaeval host. The lightly armored English, although outnumbered by five or six to one, proved superior, thanks to their organization and their archers. As the heavily armored French nobles attempted to charge across a wet plowed field, the English slaughtered over seven thousand at a cost to themselves of fewer than five hundred casualties. France was stunned, but the worst had not yet happened. While Henry occupied Normandy, the duke of Burgundy seized the French king and his government and, in 1420, in return for vast tracts ceded to himself, signed the Treaty of Troyes recognizing Henry V of England as Charles VI's heir to the throne of France.

The Dauphin, Charles, refused to accept either the treaty or his disinheritance and made good his escape from Paris to set up a rival government at Bourges. Although the young Charles was a far from promising prince, he managed to establish a semblance of authority in the south and acquired a certain popularity, perhaps because of his very weakness. With the English and their Burgundian allies in firm control north of the Loire, desultory war continued until both Henry V and Charles VI died in 1422, leaving Henry's infant son, Henry VI of England, the legal heir to the throne of France.

In October, 1428, the English mounted a major offensive against the city of Orléans in an effort to break the defensive line of the Loire protecting the southern bastion of the Dauphin. In February, 1429, when Orléans was nearing surrender and Charles's cause seemed lost, deliverance arrived in the person of Joan of Arc. A farmer's daughter from Domrémy, near the northeastern boundary of Lorraine, she had heard "voices" since childhood and had developed a local reputation for piety, prophecy, and healing. Passionately in love with France, she became obsessed with the need to expel the English and have the Dauphin crowned at Reims. By sheer obstinacy reinforced with awesome piety, Joan succeeded in persuading a local officer to take her to the Dauphin's court at Bourges. There she identified Charles, who had been disguised to test her special powers, and impressed his advisers and an ecclesiastical commission sufficiently to win permission to join the forces being mustered for the relief of Orléans. Although the claims that Joan displayed military genius in lifting the siege are quite groundless, she certainly contributed to the victory by injecting confidence into the downhearted French. Joan's appearance at Orléans was clearly the turning point; and when the English withdrew in confusion, allowing the Dauphin's forces to seize the initiative, she became the heroine of France.

Next, exploiting all her new prestige, Joan persuaded the Dauphin to go to Reims for the traditional coronation ceremony in the great cathedral of St. Remy. Although northern France was still in English hands, the French procession encountered slight resistance, and on July 17, 1429, the Dauphin, accompanied by Joan, was duly crowned Charles VII. Ten months later, in a minor skirmish, Joan was captured by the Burgundians and turned over first to the English and then to the church, to be tried for heresy. Charles made no effort on her behalf, and the trial dragged on to its inevitable and tragic denouement in her execution at the stake in Rouen on May 30, 1431. Joan's irreducible and irresistible simplicity has made her one of the great heroines of history, just as her devotion and achievements have made her the patron saint of France. Thanks to her, Charles had not only been crowned, but he had also been transformed from a puny do-nothing into a purposeful monarch; and the French had been galvanized into a nation conscious of its destiny and devoted to its king.

As Charles began to press the war, the duke of Burgundy read the signs, deserted his English allies, and made peace with his rightful king. This tipped the scales, enabling Charles to retake Paris, Rouen, Cherbourg, and Bordeaux, so that by 1453 only Calais remained in English hands. The fighting ceased, and without treaty or ceremony the Hundred Years' War finally ground to an end. Depopulated and disorganized, France lay in ruins; but the French had emerged victorious. Not only had her territory been liberated and her people's morale restored, but her monarch, sanctified by Joan's revival of the mediaeval mystique of kingship, was able to lead the nation, reinvigorated by her evocation of a new patriotism, toward recovery and the foundation of a vigorous national monarchy.

In the course of his long reign (1422–1461), Charles and his able advisers succeeded in developing and transforming the royal institutions in the direction of greater administrative independence from, and authority over, the feudal elements of the realm. Fundamental to the whole program was the laying down of a modern financial base. The crown established its permanent right to "extraordinary" revenues, to the continuation in peacetime of the special taxes which had been exacted to finance the war. Thus, to the king's traditional "ordinary" revenues from royal estates and customary taxes were added the gabelle on salt, the *aide* on sales, and most significant, the taille on land or hearths—all transformed into annual levies. With such impressive new resources, Charles was able to create a standing army. Through a series of military ordinances issued between 1439 and 1451, he suppressed the unruly free companies which had wreaked such havoc during the Hundred Years' War and arrogated to himself the exclusive right of raising troops. By creating a professional officer corps of nobles to command a strictly disciplined army stationed in permanent provincial garrisons, the king was able to put down uprisings and bring to heel such grandees as the dukes of Bourbon, Orléans, and Alençon. Even the church felt the impact of the royal power. By the Pragmatic Sanction, promulgated at Bourges in 1438, the king had subordinated papal authority and revenue to his control and had made himself virtual head of the church in France.

Impressive as his accomplishments were, Charles VII left many unresolved and urgent problems to his son and successor, Louis XI (1461–1483). Tagged the "Spider King" by history, Louis was a strange, neurotic personality, treacherous, deceitful, and cruel, but single-minded and tenacious in his devotion to the monarchy he had inherited. Sometimes mistakenly described as "modern," he was in fact as mediaeval as his contemporaries, but of a bourgeois rather than an aristocratic turn of mind.

Delighted at the news of his father's death and his own consequent succession, Louis rushed to Paris and threw himself into the business of being king. More than any of his predecessors, he based his power on the support of his towns, particularly Paris, and avoided fighting for anything he could buy. Allegedly, his passion for bribery extended to attempts to buy the intervention of saints through lavish votive offerings. His chief opponents and bitterest enemies were, inevitably, the great nobles, who in 1465 formed the League of the Public Weal to defend their threatened interests. If they failed ultimately to subordinate the monarchy to their control, largely through lack of leadership and discipline, they nevertheless made such inroads against the king's authority that it took Louis years to recover from their insubordination and repeated armed attacks. Gradually, however, he brought these princely antagonists under control. One by one, the dukes of Brittany, Anjou, and Maine and the counts of Armagnac and Foix were either eliminated or subjugated and their fiefs and appanages returned to royal jurisdiction, until only Charles of Burgundy remained in open defiance of the crown.

Although Louis eventually manipulated the downfall of this last among his great rivals, he did so at the cost of creating still other problems. Having formed a coalition with the Empire and the Swiss, the king brought the contumacious duke to defeat and death in 1477; but at this moment of apparent triumph Louis saw his ally, the wily Emperor Maximilian, make off with Charles's daughter Mary and the bulk of the Burgundian inheritance. The obvious menace this marriage created for the king of France was compounded by still another wedding, that of Ferdinand and Isabella. That the first would open a bitter rivalry with the Hapsburgs was understood by everyone, but no one dreamed that the newly united Spain was also destined to become a possession of the Hapsburgs, and therefore, no one foresaw the full consequences for the French.

In spite of his failure to prevent the Spanish union,

Louis proved himself a remarkably successful king. Having consolidated the great fiefs of the monarchy, he reduced the towns and cities to subservience. By transforming municipal officers into royal agents, he vastly increased the size and efficiency of his bureaucracy and succeeded in quadrupling his revenues. Thus, by working with the wealthy bourgeois to maintain order, revive business, and restore prosperity, he managed to win their support while he was increasing their tax load by fiscal innovations. Altogether, Louis XI made remarkable progress toward the centralization of the royal administration and the development of the absolute authority of the king.

Under his successors, Charles VIII (1483–1498) and Louis XII (1498–1515), the consolidation of the royal powers continued. The *conseil du roi*, composed of the chief administrative officers of the realm, gradually absorbed such traditional prerogatives of the old estates, or provincial assemblies, as the right to impose taxes or name a regent. The estates-general, representing the entire kingdom, were summoned less and less frequently; and where popular support was needed, the crown resorted increasingly to the more tractable provincial estates, such as those in Languedoc and Brittany. Similarly, the *grand conseil*, which included princes as well as bureaucrats, also displaced the estates as a judicial body and became a sort of supreme court by extending its jurisdiction to all cases of special interest to the king and making its judgements immune to appeal. At the same time the provincial courts, or parlements, staffed by bourgeois lawyers, not only survived but actually gained in authority. Thus, as the bureaucratic power of the absolute monarchy expanded at the expense of traditional institutions, notably the estates-general, certain local, even semiautonomous, agencies were developed by royal support, creating the peculiar relationship of local government to the central administration which was to become a principal characteristic of the *ancien régime.*

Both Charles VIII and Louis XII nourished dreams of military glory, and both inherited claims to the kingdom of Naples from their Angevin ancestors. With this lure added to the traditional fantasy of liberating Constantinople from the infidel and restoring its Christian empire, Charles VIII invaded Italy in 1494. As might have been expected, his attack on Naples brought the Spanish sovereigns into the struggle in support, not merely of their Aragonese cousin (the king of Naples), but in defense of their own very active interests in western Mediterranean trade. In addition, but less predictably, the Hapsburgs joined what thus became a formidable— and ultimately successful—military coalition striving for control of the Italian peninsula. To some, this confused thirty-five-year struggle has seemed to mark the beginning of modern "international" politics. Domination, as Lord Acton pointed out, became a reigning motive in European history, for which a monarch would sacrifice all the resources of his kingdom. The new national states, unwilling to tolerate either limitations on their own ambitions or the fulfillment of those of their neighbors, lived in a condition of internecine competition for conquest and survival, nowhere more deadly than on the peninsula of Italy.

England

Like France and Spain, England at the beginning of the fifteenth century was divided and weak, but in spite of disasters and disorders, she managed to emerge strong and united. In this island kingdom, however, where the monarchy could not justify a standing army for self-defense, the mediaeval parliament retained control of revenues and legislation. Although the kings did gain great strength, they never became as autocratic as their rivals on the Continent. Furthermore, it must be remembered that once shorn of her continental possessions, as she was after mid-century, England was much smaller, less populous, and therefore poorer than either France or Spain. Until long after the opening of the Atlantic, she remained on the periphery of European trade, culture, and even politics. But her later importance as a world leader makes the events of this, her formative period, of utmost interest.

Henry of Lancaster, having deposed the last of the Plantagenets, justified his seizure of the throne by claims based on inheritance, conquest, and parliamentary support; but the struggle between the new Henry IV (1399–1413) and his nobles did not cease with his coronation. In practice, this meant that the royal council continued to exercise authority, while the burghers and gentry worked in Parliament to restrain and direct royal spending. Not feeling sufficiently secure to challenge this opposition by imposing basic reforms on governmental procedures, Henry IV was forced to cut expenses. To this end he let the war with France lapse, thus dissembling rather than abandoning his ambitions, and thereby merely delaying the inevitable disaster.

The young Henry V (1413–1422) dazzled the English with his announcement to the French that he intended to claim their throne and make good his promise to lead a crusade to "build again the walls of Jerusalem." In

response to Henry's appeal to the emerging national consciousness of his subjects, the nobles put aside political
quarrels, the burghers forgot economic problems, and
the country united in preparation for the impending war.
At the same time, with unprecedented diplomatic skill
Henry kept the Burgundians and the Emperor friendly
and English trade safe. In a lightning invasion, he nearly
annihilated the French nobility at Agincourt, married
the French Princess Catherine, and had himself declared
heir to the throne of France. When he suddenly died of
camp fever near Paris, while still attempting to make
good his claims after seven years of struggle, Henry V
had raised English prestige on the Continent but had
notably failed to contribute to the development of effective government at home.

His nine-month-old son was proclaimed Henry VI of
England in 1422 and two months later, following the
death of his maternal grandfather, Charles VI, was recognized as king of France as well. As Henry approached
maturity, however, it became apparent that he had
inherited from his French grandfather not only his crown
but his insanity as well. Throughout his reign, the fortunes of England declined abroad as rapidly as those of
the throne did at home. When, by 1453, the English were
finally expelled from all of France except Calais, they
seemed to repatriate all the strife and disorder they had
sown abroad, with the demented king's rapacious uncles
and cousins conniving and contending with the royal
council and the Parliament and unleashing anarchy
throughout the land.

Many of England's difficulties were created by social
and economic changes. Ancient institutions founded on
reciprocal services and loyalties had become anachronis-

tic in the new secular and mercenary age. Attempts to adapt the traditional institutions ended by producing what has been called "bastard feudalism." The monarchy was reduced to using tax money to pay the great nobles vast sums, ostensibly for the military services of their "companies" but in reality as bribes for their "support." Thus enabled to reach beyond their fiefs to hire enough retainers and troops to challenge the authority of the crown itself, the magnates developed into English counterparts of the *ricos hombres* in Spain, the appanage lords in France, and the independent princes in Germany and Italy. The basis of this new power was the reciprocal relationship between the lords and their retainers, formalized in contracts by which the former promised to defend or "maintain" the interests of the latter in litigation—that is, to overawe even royal courts by appearing in force at the head of their retainers—in return for which the same retainers agreed to wear the lords' livery and serve them upon their summons.

In England, where the lack of a standing army left the king dependent on feudal levies for military support, this practice of "livery and maintenance," as it was called, threatened the very existence of public law and order. The defeat in France coupled with misgovernment at court robbed the monarchy of all confidence and respect. Throughout the period, contemporaries appealed for reform, or more "abundant government," as from place to place popular discontent grew into open revolt. In 1450 rebellious peasants captured the city of London, and for some time no one seemed able or willing to take the lead in restoring order.

The stage was set for civil war. The traditional rivalry among the king's own relatives for control of the council deteriorated into a naked contest for the throne; and the House of York opened a campaign to supplant the Lancastrian line by advancing legal claims to the royal inheritance. Then, in 1455, two years after the expulsion of the English from France had flooded England with "companies" of unemployed mercenaries, both sides took to arms. Virtually all the <u>nobles joined one faction or the other, not to uphold constitutional principles, but to further private feuds and interests.</u> Though the middle and lower classes remained largely indifferent and inactive, these deadly Wars of the Roses, as they have traditionally been called, dragged on for thirty years.

Edward, duke of York, finally brought temporary order out of the endemic chaos by deposing Henry VI and proclaiming himself king. As Edward IV (1461–1483), he was able to restore a degree of royal authority and financial solvency and to deal successfully with several Lancastrian uprisings, one of which briefly restored Henry VI in 1471. The reconstruction begun by this Yorkist king was terminated by his death in 1483, and England was plunged once again into civil war. Edward's twelve-year-old son sat briefly on the throne as Edward V, until his shrewd but neurotic uncle, the duke of Gloucester, consigned him and his brother to the Tower of London. Then, having seized the crown as Richard III (1483–1485), the usurper—who was immortalized by Shakespeare as an archetypal monster and tyrant but who has been somewhat exonerated by modern scholars —succeeded in raising more opposition than support. The widely accepted charge that he had had the little princes murdered roused dissident elements to rally around the latest Lancastrian claimant, Henry Tudor, duke of Richmond. With the defeat and death of

Richard on Bosworth Field in 1485, Henry brought the House of York and the Wars of the Roses to an end.

Henry VII (1485–1509), the able if little-known victor, founded the new Tudor dynasty and began the restoration and transformation of the monarchy. To strengthen his political position, he married Elizabeth, eldest daughter of Edward IV, and to symbolize the significance of this union of the Lancastrian and Yorkist factions, he had her crowned in a rich and solemn ceremony. In time he gained still more prestige by marrying his eldest son to Catherine of Aragon, the daughter of Ferdinand and Isabella, and his daughter Margaret to James IV of Scotland. In spite of these brilliant foreign marriages, Henry still had to suppress repeated factional attempts to undermine his position at home.

Although England's once powerful mediaeval monarchy appeared to be disintegrating, much of its bureaucratic institutional machinery still existed in a moribund condition. To bring the institutions back to vigorous life, the Tudors discovered, they had only to reassert the personal authority that had made all mediaeval prerogative effective. Moreover, since the general population had suffered relatively little loss of property during the civil disorders, the nation needed only peace and secure government to flourish once again.

Henry VII's most remarkable achievement was his reorganization of the royal finances. He assiduously milked all the traditional sources of the crown—royal income, customs duties, feudal dues, and ecclesiastical revenues—while keeping a close check on government expenditure. But no king of the time, not even the frugal Henry, could hope to "live on his own," and he was forced to develop new expedients. One that was to cause bitter resentment was the shameless exploitation of his right to impose fines and grant pardons for the slightest misdemeanors or "dead letter" crimes. In addition to seeking new sources of revenue by such dubious means, he also strove to reduce expenses both by improving methods of accounting and by cutting unnecessary outlay, particularly for military forces on land and sea.

To the remarkable feat of refinancing the monarchy without seriously increasing fiscal exactions from the populace, Henry VII added the inspired accomplishment of making Parliament a cooperative, if not complaisant, partner of the crown. Further, he cultivated the support and loyalty of the commercial elements of the realm by promoting prosperity and increasing foreign trade. But he kept the reins of government firmly in his own grasp. His chief administrative instrument, the royal council, was composed of the great officers of state and household ministers who enforced the ordinance, supervised finances, and conducted embassies abroad. This council, in some ways resembling a modern cabinet, also began to sit regularly as a high court of virtually unlimited authority—the English counterpart of the Audiencia in Castile and the judicial section of the *conseil du roi* in France. Known as the Court of Star Chamber, because of its meeting place, it acquired an awesome reputation for dealing effectively with "over-mighty subjects." Various other sub-bodies, with special duties, gradually took on the appearance of separate institutions, but such definition was slow and never absolute. The whole growth of the administration, always dictated by convenience, represented the gradual hardening of expedients into precedents and the proliferation of an unpremeditated system.

Summary

In the fifteenth century, two great new political phenomena almost completely transformed the political life of western and west-central Europe. Both centralized administration and national consciousness emerged with the development of new states. The one gave sinew and the other spirit of these evolving monarchies, enabling their kings and princes to establish dynasties and pursue territorial consolidation with the services of trained bureaucrats and disciplined armies, as well as with the enthusiastic support of that new element "the people." A kind of national union under popular dynasties was achieved, not only in Spain, France, and England, but also in Burgundy and regions of Italy and Germany. Most surviving feudal magnates had to submit to the new sovereigns, although a few, such as the Bourbons in France and the bishops of Durham in England, managed to preserve substantial elements of independence. The ordinary nobles, however, lost purpose as well as power while the bourgeois, making tremendous gains in status and self-confidence, increasingly replaced them in royal administration. It was the monarchs, however, who made the greatest gains and whose appetite for power increased the most. Thus, during the fifteenth century a great deal had been done to expand the jurisdiction as well as increase the authority of monarchical government on all levels, but gargantuan tasks remained for the future builders of the modern state. In western and west-central Europe the ultimate triumph of the prince and *raison d'état* over the feudal lords and chivalry was by 1500 inevitable though still incomplete.

Eastern Europe

CHAPTER IV

Political Patterns East

EASTERN Europe, in both its history and geography, contrasted sharply with the West. Because of poorer climate, soil, and topography, the East was underdeveloped. The population of the Balkan Peninsula, tied more to the Mediterranean than to the Continent, had followed the lead of Byzantium; but the peoples that inhabited the cold plains of eastern Europe lagged far behind and only slowly came to develop monarchies, accept Christianity, and even use the plow. If, however, they had contributed little to the advance of civilization before 1300, during the next 150 years they nearly overtook their neighbors to the west.

During the fourteenth and early fifteenth centuries, when western and west-central Europe, in the grip of famine, plague, and wars, seemed on the point of economic and political disintegration, the lands between the (1300-1450) Elbe and the Dnieper prospered. For the first time this area played a positive role in the history of western civilization. A great agricultural expansion stimulated the growth of towns, and those along the seacoasts and rivers began trading with the commercial cities of the

Mediterranean and North Sea, as well as with the caravan
junctions on the steppes. The old urban economy of west-
central Europe seemed to be shifting to the east, and by
1400, Poland, Bohemia, and Hungary appeared to be
emerging as rivals of England, France, and Castile. But
when the hard-hit West finally began to revive and trade
moved increasingly out into the Atlantic, the East once
more fell behind, never again to challenge the economic
pre-eminence of its better-place rivals.

Those local rulers in east-central Europe who had been
trying to take advantage of the economic boom to emulate
the rising monarchs of the West ultimately failed in their
efforts to create centralized kingdoms. The towns, whose
counterparts were proving such vigorous allies of royal
authority in the West, never became strong enough to
play the same decisive role. As a result, the eastern kings
had none of the basic elements of power necessary to
subjugate their nobility or to integrate them into effective
bureaucracies or standing armies. Even the many local
magnates, who transformed their traditional position as
tribal chieftains into the more independent status of
feudal lords, were unable to form stable principalities.
Their one important success was defensive. By uniting
in representative estates, or diets, they were able to resist
the efforts of would-be monarchs to give new substance
to old legends of once powerful kingdoms. Though a few
monarchs survived as figureheads, they found no significant class or segment of the population to support their
pretensions. Even the peasants lacked the ethnic, linguistic, and religious homogeneity that was contributing to
the new sense of national identity in various parts of the
West. Only along the eastern frontier did strong states
emerge; but both the Grand Duchy of Muscovy and the

Ottoman Empire were more Oriental and despotic in character than European and feudal. Geography and history thus again conspired to retard the political and economic development of eastern Europe.

Geography, Peoples, and Religions

Eastern Europe has always been as much a cultural as a geographic concept. Though its traditional eastern boundary is the Urals, in the west it is defined by the line that divides predominantly Slavic ethnic and linguistic areas from the Germanic or Italian territories of central Europe. In the north this division is effected by the Baltic and in the south by the Adriatic. The line connecting the two seas is bent toward the west by the Harz and Bohemian Mountains that define Bohemia, and then toward the east by the upper Danube Valley that thrusts beyond Vienna to the famous Iron Gate formed by the eastern Alps and western Carpathians that meet at the river. For those familiar with the map of Europe in the second half of the twentieth century, this line will be readily recognizable as the "curtain" between Soviet satellites and the West—with only the single difference that since the 1200's East Germany was considered part of western Europe.

Even where these boundaries were geographical in character they offered no serious impediment to migration and, since time immemorial, invaders have swept into the great central plain that constitutes the bulk of the area. The vast forest areas in the north and west and the Carpathian and Balkan Mountains in the southeast served primarily to slow the westward advance and to precipitate population deposits that produced a complex of linguistic, ethnic, and eventually cultural units.

Although these groups were not separated by well-defined boundaries, by the end of the Middle Ages they formed a pattern that is still recognizable today.

During the great migrations of the early Middle Ages, Slavic-speaking peoples came to populate most of eastern Europe. Three basic groups evolved: the Western Slavs, settled in a triangular area with its apex thrusting westward into the Bohemian plateau; the Southern Slavs, based between the Danube River and the Balkan Mountains; and finally the Eastern Slavs, or Russians, located in what is today European Russia. In time each split into subgroups speaking distinct languages: the Western Slavs into Wends, Sorbs, Poles, Czechs, and Slovaks; the Eastern Slavs into Great Russians, White Russians, and Little Russians, (the last were also known as Ukrainians or Ruthenians); and the Southern Slavs into Macedonians, Slovenes, Serbs, and Croats.

Non-Slavic peoples had also gained a place in eastern Europe by the end of the early Middle Ages. Five of them spoke Finno-Ugric languages. Of these the Finns, in the extreme north, and the Estonians, Livs, and Cours, just south of the Gulf of Finland, lived on the eastern shores of the Baltic, while the Magyars occupied the center of the Danube Valley. Another major non-Slavic linguistic group—the Letts, Lithuanians, and Prussians, known collectively as Balts—was strung out along the southern shore of the Baltic Sea. Along the lower Danube, in what is now Rumania, the Vlachs, probably descended—at least in part—from Roman settlers, spoke a Romance language derived from Latin. To the south of them, the Bulgars, in spite of their Mongol origin, had adopted a Slavic language, while at the southern end of the Balkan Peninsula the Greeks, though mixed with Slavic immigrants, continued to speak their own language. To complete the list, it is necessary to mention those survivors from earlier migrations who still inhabited a small mountainous area along the Adriatic and spoke Albanian. In the early Middle Ages, the western Latin and the eastern Greek churches had competed for the conversion of the indigenous pagan population. The Greek rite was established among the Serbs, the Bulgars, the Vlachs, and all the Eastern Slavs; but the Latin ritual triumphed among the Croats, the Slovenes, the Magyars, the Finns, and almost all the Western Slavs. Thus, by 1100 the division between the Orthodox and Catholic religions, together with that between the Greek and Latin cultures, split eastern Europe down the middle; and the few remaining pagans—the Balts, Wends, Estonians, Livs, and Cours—would, before the end of the Middle Ages, be forced to choose between Catholicism and extinction. The line of religious cleavage, it might be noted, coincides strikingly with that formed by the eastern boundaries of the new states that appeared in central Europe following the First World War. Running between Finland and the Soviet Union in the north, it followed the Russian boundary, deviating only to take in part of Poland and most of Yugoslavia and the Balkans, thus establishing an effective division between east-central and eastern Europe.

Between the twelfth and the fourteenth centuries invaders overran almost all of eastern Europe: the Teutons from the west, the Mongols from the east, and the Turks from the south. Only Poland-Lithuania, Bohemia, and Hungary—all three in the central part of the region—managed to maintain their independence. Around them the invaders' domination left a lasting imprint. Thus, by the fifteenth century the Finns, Estonians, and Balts were largely reduced to the status of serfs of German or Swedish nobles. At the same time the Southern Slavs, Greeks, Albanians, and Vlachs were being conquered by the Turks, while most of the Russians, or Eastern Slavs, were still suffering, or just emerging from, Mongol domination.

The history of eastern Europe, then, in the fifteenth— or first modern—century is confused. The still independent Western Slavs and Magyars fought on all sides to defend themselves. The Poles and Lithuanians not only stopped the German advance in the northwest, but they actually drove it back in places. The Czechs became involved in a long struggle for independence against their German rulers; and in the south and southeast the Hungarians resisted the intermittent but powerful pressure of the Turks, to which most of the South Slavs had already succumbed. In the east and northeast the pattern exhibited a strange variation. There the Eastern Slavs, or Russians, adopting the ambitions and even to some extent the methods of their recent Mongol lords, began the cautious but relentless drive that was eventually (in our own day) to make them masters of the entire area. But for most of the fifteenth century, the Russians still had to rely on intermittent and independent forays of their western neighbors to maintain pressure on the Mongols.

The principal actors in this story, therefore, are the Poles, Lithuanians, Czechs, and Hungarians; and its geographical focus is the western sector of the great plain extending from the southern shores of the Baltic to the Balkan and Carpathian Mountains and from the Bohemian Mountains in the west to the valley of the Dnieper in the east. The ill-defined and loosely organized kingdoms gradually learned to coordinate their efforts against their common enemies, frequently through electing the same leader king of more than one country, thus creating personal monarchical unions. The fact that these eastern kingdoms were so loosely organized undoubtedly contributed to the ease with which they formed these combinations. The attempts of the various kings during the fourteenth century to imitate the centralizing efforts of their fellow sovereigns in the west had not quite succeeded. In spite of their new prosperity, they were still basically dependent on the voluntary support of their nobles; and while this was usually forthcoming in any crisis caused by foreign invasion, it frequently cost constitutional concessions. The inevitable result was the reduction of these emergent kings to mere figurehead rulers of decentralized aristocratic republics. To follow these developments, it will be necessary to consider the history of each area in turn.

East-central Europe

Viewed from our vantage point in the West, the story begins in the twelfth century, when the Germans began to push permanent settlements across the Elbe. Extending their influence or domination to eastern Europe in a continuing movement that has become famous as the *Drang nach Osten*, their conquest, though frequently directed by prelates or religious orders, was brutal. The Slavic peoples living between the Elbe and the Oder, usually referred to as the Wends and the Sorbs, almost completely disappeared under the impact, and their territory was divided among powerful bishops, abbots, and lay lords. The Prussians, too, began to vanish from the area as the Teutonic Knights, a military order originally organized to fight in the Holy Land, transferred their operations to the shores of the Baltic in 1229. Gradually pushing their conquest east, they exterminated those inhabitants they failed to Germanize and absorb. Simultaneously other Germans—nobles, clerics, and townsmen —subjugated but did not assimilate the indigenous population of the rest of the southern shore of the Baltic, in Livonia, Courland, and Estonia.

In other areas—Poland, Lithuania, Bohemia, and Hungary—strong native princes fiercely resisted conquest but encouraged peaceful German immigration, hoping to benefit economically from the new settlers. As a result two border areas—Silesia, a Polish-speaking province on the upper Oder, and what has become known to Americans as the Sudetenland, the mountainous region on the Czech side of the German frontier—were largely Germanized. In addition, Transylvania, a rich agricultural region protected by mountains, also received a particularly heavy German influx. Unlike the Asiatic invaders of eastern Europe, the Germans were townspeople who brought skills, industries, and a highly developed culture as well. Thanks to these contributions, they tended to dominate the scattered towns in which they settled and to exert disproportionate influence in the churches and the courts. In consequence they fostered all too natural resentment and resistance among the indigenous rural population, both gentry and peasants, of these eastern kingdoms.

The only political entities in eastern Europe to maintain their independence were the Christian kingdoms of Poland, Bohemia, and Hungary, and the still pagan Grand Duchy of Lithuania. For a while, it looked as if these might also succumb—Poland and Bohemia to the Germans, Hungary to the Turks, and Lithuania to the

Tartars. Rallied by brilliant leaders in the fourteenth and
fifteenth centuries, however, these countries not only
survived but flourished as never before. Able to tap the
wealth of the expanding agriculture and the prosperous
new towns, these rulers succeeded in establishing bases
of central authority from which they moved first to rein-
force their threatened frontiers and then to challenge
simultaneously their own entrenched nobles and clergy
and their threatening neighbors. So fiercely did the native
magnates oppose the administrative ambitions of the
kings, however, that by the end of the fifteenth century
the forces that would normally have contributed to the
centralization of royal power had been weakened and
diverted by their efforts to stop the Turks. Distracted by
their temporary success in this campaign and urged on
by their nobles, the kings proceeded to mount victorious
counteroffensives against the Germans and the Tartars;
but in the process their authority within their monarchies
was seriously eroded. By the end of the century all the
thrones in east-central Europe had been reduced to the
status of elective offices. In spite of these struggles, or
because of apparent victories, the later Middle Ages
seemed to mark a high point in the development of
Poland, Bohemia, Hungary, and Lithuania, and—in more
recent, less happy times—their peoples have tended to
look back on this period as a golden age.

Poland and Lithuania

By 1300, Poland was still little more than a "geographical expression" denoting the valley of the Vistula. A
sprawling, sparsely populated rural country with ill-
defined and fluctuating borders, it consisted of only three
provinces: Great Poland, Lesser Poland, and Masovia.

Silesia, still populated predominantly by Poles in spite of the heavy German immigration, had fallen to Bohemia. The Teutonic Knights ruled western as well as eastern Prussia, thus controlling the mouth of the Vistula and Poland's access to the sea. To resist this foreign threat, Casimir the Great (1333–1370), the last of the Piast dynasty which had ruled Poland since the tenth century, set out to strengthen his kingdom through a program of reforms. He managed to codify Polish law, then to create a rudimentary central administration, check the unruly nobles, attract migrant peasants, and encourage the growth of cities. He even founded the University of Cracow, which antedated any German university and which, in the sixteenth century, was to produce the great Copernicus. He also induced refugee Jews from the west to come and settle in such numbers that Poland eventually had the largest Jewish population in the world. Before these farsighted efforts could produce sufficient returns to enable him to establish an independent administrative authority, however, he died.

His brother-in-law and successor, Louis the Great (1370–1382) of Hungary, was able to win election to the throne only by promising the nobles a strong voice in political affairs and virtual control of all taxation. This set a fateful precedent according to which the diet, now the stronghold of the nobility, regularly wrung concessions from aspiring candidates to the crown. Its upper chamber, or Senate, was the king's council and consisted of the great magnates, much as did its western prototypes. The lower house, however, instead of representing the towns, whose dominant patriciate was non-Polish, was composed largely of delegates from provincial legislatures which were entirely dominated by the local nobles. After the death of Louis, the magnates elected his daughter,

Jadwiga, "king" (since the constitution had no provision for a queen) and married her to the pagan Jagello, Grand Duke of Lithuania. Following his conversion to Roman Catholicism, he too was named king of Poland, thus uniting the two countries under a single dynasty.

Lithuania, before its union with Poland, had been the largest, though by no means the best organized, realm in Europe. Its size was due in part to the instinctive respect of its ruling class for local rights and customs. For example, Lithuanian magnates not only tolerated but occasionally actually adopted the Orthodox faith and culture, and in some cases even the language, of the White Russians and Ukranians they were annexing in the wake of the Mongol withdrawal. Not surprisingly, therefore, other Russian states—Tver in particular—had sometimes sought the protection of these moderate, if quite unorthodox, Lithuanians against the Orthodox but despotic Muscovites. Even so, the Lithuanians, most of whom remained pagan until Jagello's conversion, were encircled by hostile powers: Poles, Teutonic Knights, Muscovites, Turks, and Tartars. Their primitive tribal structure, religious differences, and failure to practice primogeniture encouraged internal disorders, which in turn rendered their military position precarious. Rival Lithuanian princes eventually invited the Teutonic Knights to intervene in their domestic conflicts; and in 1389, Grand Duke Jagello turned, in desperation, to his old rivals the Poles, who, also threatened by the Knights, were ready to make common cause and sanction his marriage with Jadwiga.

As the last stronghold of paganism in Europe, Lithuania had long been a prime target of the Knights. These incorrigible crusaders, having won the Baltic littoral for Catholicism, intended to convert and dominate its Lithuanian hinterland and annex some Polish provinces into the bargain. In pursuit of these objectives they were all but annihilated, in 1410, by the combined armies of Poland and Lithuania led by Jagello and his cousin the legendary hero Vitold. The battle of Grunwald, or Tannenberg, which in effect opened the fifteenth-century phase of the history of this area, broke the military power of the Knights, who had already lost their religious *raison d'être* as a result of the conversion of the Lithuanians. Thus weakened, the Knights also found their hold on Prussia threatened by class strife and social revolts. The war dragged on, however, until the Knights suffered another defeat and ceded the valley of the lower Vistula in the Second Peace of Thorn, in 1466. Thus ended three centuries of German encroachment on the Slavs. In spite of Polish control of this "corridor" through German territory, however, the rich port of Danzig continued to be ruled and to be largely populated by Germans, who kept alive a smoldering hostility against, as well as a feeling of superiority to, the surrounding Slavs.

In the fourteenth century, the still rival kingdoms of Poland and Lithuania had begun to expand toward the east to fill the vacuum left by the Mongol retreat. Then, strengthened by the dynastic union arranged at the end of the century, Poland seized Galicia; and Lithuania, after incorporating White Russia, managed to secure most of the Ukraine and control of the north shore of the Black Sea as far east as the no man's land separating her outposts from the Tartars. She even dominated Moscow itself during the minority of one grand duke, thus approaching the fulfillment of her long-cherished dream of controlling all Eastern Slavs. But though the union had improved Lithuania's position in foreign affairs, it had also contributed to the creation of new and serious domestic problems.

First, the decentralization of royal power, already well advanced in the Polish diet, continued under the united monarchy until it reached its ultimate conclusion, in 1505, in the famous constitution *Nihil Novi* (Nothing New). Its provisions further restricted the prerogatives of the crown and increased those of the nobles by promising that nothing new would be decreed without the unanimous consent of both houses of the diet. In practice this meant that the negative vote of a single delegate, the famous *liberum veto*, could block any piece of legislation. Thereafter, the power of the kings depended almost entirely on their vast agricultural wealth or their personal magnetism.

Second, many of the upper-class Lithuanians became Catholic, while most of their subjects, the majority of whom were Eastern Slavs, remained Orthodox. Thus new religious differences, accentuating old ethnic divisions, created a fatal political weakness in the Polish-Lithuanian state and provided Moscow with the invaluable role of defender of the Orthodox faith. Late in the century, Ivan III of Moscow launched an attack on Lithuanian territory in the Ukraine and White Russia which, in spite of pauses and setbacks, was to culminate in the famous eighteenth-century partitions of Poland. By means of these notorious arrangements the German-speaking rulers of Prussia and Austria absorbed the western parts of Poland-Lithuania, and Ivan's Russian successors took most of the area that had been united in 1389, including even the basin of the Vistula.

Bohemia

Early in the fourteenth century the Bohemian throne had devolved upon pro-Czech princes of the House of Luxemburg. In 1346, Bohemia's king, Charles IV, was elected Holy Roman Emperor. His interest, however, continued to center in Bohemia, to which the original Premysl dynasty had attached the margravate of Moravia, the Lusatias, and Silesia; in the latter two, Germans and Poles outnumbered Czechs. Wishing to strengthen his hereditary possessions, Charles attempted to incorporate these new acquisitions with Bohemia in a firm dynastic union, but his plan aroused vigorous local opposition.

Even his famous Golden Bull of 1356, ostensibly intended as a new basis for imperial policy, was fashioned to favor the interests of Bohemia. Not only did this act assure to the seven imperial electors complete legal immunity from political interference, but it also gave the king of Bohemia, as chief elector, a preponderant influence in German affairs. Moreover, by transforming Prague into a great and beautiful city with archbishopric and university, Charles made it the effective capital of the Empire and one of the intellectual centers of Europe.

Bohemia itself, in spite of greater ethnic homogeneity than any other kingdom in east-central Europe, contained sizable German minorities, particularly in the Sudetenland. In addition, many of the nobles, clerics, and burghers spoke German, a situation that created chronic misunderstanding and hostility in the Slavic-speaking peasantry. Open conflict between these two groups finally flared under Wenceslas (1378–1419), Charles's eldest son, who succeeded his father on both the imperial and Bohemian thrones. Although he was deposed from the former in 1400, he continued to reign in Bohemia, until Prague erupted in a national revolt against the Germans. In the reigns of both Charles and Wenceslas many Czechs had been attracted to the capital. Like most cities of eastern Europe, it was composed of an "old town" largely populated by Germans and a "new town" inhabited by Slavs. The inevitable tension between the overbearing German patriciate and the new Czech majority was soon kindled into civil religious war by a charismatic leader.

A professor of theology, John Hus won popular support through his denunciations of the corruption of the higher clergy and the pretensions of the papacy. Once he began attacking the influence of foreign groups within Bohemia, the German members of the university retaliated by refusing to support Wenceslas' plan to end the papal schism. Thus challenged, the king deprived the Germans of their voting control of the faculty, and in protest they left to found the University of Leipzig. Thereupon, Wenceslas made Hus rector of the University of Prague. When, by order of the Council of Constance, Hus was burned for heresy in 1415, most Czechs, irrespective of class or condition, rose in revolt. The uprising was national (against the Germans), social (against the rich), and religious (against the decadent and divided church); but its immediate target was the German elite, which enjoyed a disproportionate share of the nation's worldly wealth and clerical power. With the death of Wenceslas in 1419 and the spontaneous refusal of the Czechs to accept his staunchly Catholic brother, Emperor Sigismund, as his successor on the Bohemian throne, the uprising was transformed into civil war.

The Hussite Wars not only threatened to split Bohemia along religious lines but also to break off its incorporated provinces. (See below, Chapter V.) The Hussites repelled two crusades hurled against them and launched a counteroffensive that ravaged much of central Europe; but before they could consolidate their military gains, they fell victims to internal dissension. Frightened by the emergence within their ranks of a minority of poor radicals, the majority of the Hussites turned on and exterminated these visionary extremists. In an effort to defend social stability against their revolutionary brethren, the majority negotiated a settlement with their conservative opponents. Because they agreed to recognize the papacy and Sigismund, they were allowed to retain certain religious practices, especially the right of the laity to partake of the wine as well as the bread in the ceremony of Communion. This was considered particularly important because it symbolized to them their emancipation from the foreign clergy. A confused interregnum followed Sigismund's death, until a Czech nobleman, the former regent, George Podiebrad (1458–1471), was finally elevated to the throne. A moderate Hussite and a popular leader, Podiebrad took vigorous steps to restore the monarchy; but during his reign a new extremist Hussite group, called the Czech or Moravian Brethren, rejected his leadership and withdrew from the Roman church. Roused to vengeance, the Pope repeatedly incited its neighbors to crush Bohemia. Finally the king of Hungary launched an invasion. Before Podiebrad could re-establish order, he died and was succeeded by Ladislas Jagello (1471–1516). This son of the Polish sovereign managed, after restoring an uneasy peace in Bohemia, to win election to the throne of Hungary and to unite the warring kingdoms by a common dynasty with Poland. Calm was finally restored to the realm, but at the cost of heavy royal concessions to the nobility and clergy. Worse still, from the point of view of Czech nationalists, the crown had passed into unsympathetic foreign hands, going to the Jagellons in 1471 and then to the Hapsburgs in 1526.

Devastated by the Hussite struggles, foreign invasions,

weak kings, and frequent changes of dynasty, the royal power had been so eroded in Bohemia that the diet had been able to follow the Polish precedent and establish the principle of an <u>elective monarchy</u>.

Rival candidates for the kingship were regularly forced to pledge the crown's prerogatives and resources in advance, and the victor was even sometimes compelled to dissipate them further in order to retain the throne after his election. Such was the general anarchy that ensued that <u>even the great lords suffered. The lesser nobles and the burghers, who dominated the Hussite armies and the diets, were able to encroach on the interests of the magnates and prelates on the one hand and of the peasants and laborers on the other.</u> Instead of supporting their sovereigns, they strove for personal autonomy. The Czech monarchy itself suffered most severely from the confusion. Salvaging only fragments of past national greatness, it entered a period of severe decline and only lingered on until it was destroyed in the Thirty Years' War.

Under Hussite patronage, the Czech language developed into a literary vernacular, and the more radical theological ideas of Hus were cultivated at home and propagated abroad. Although any direct effect of these proselytizing efforts would be virtually impossible to measure, it is interesting to note that Martin Luther was born and lived less than a hundred miles from the Bohemian frontier.

Hungary

Lying exposed in the middle of the Danube Basin, Hungary has never enjoyed the security often provided, or suffered the restriction often imposed, by natural frontiers. During the high Middle Ages, the native Arpad dynasty expanded its rule in every direction, annexing Croatia to the west, Transylvania to the east, Slovakia to the north, and the Banat to the south. These disparate areas, each with its own language, customs, and religious convictions, were bundled together to form a greater Hungary; but instead of merging, their inhabitants persevered as recalcitrant minorities. The ethnopolitical situation was further complicated by Germans and Jews who moved down the Danube to settle in the cities and in Transylvania. Although the Arpads had managed to Catholicize their Magyar subjects, they failed to consolidate their overextended kingdom or to disengage it from territorial struggles with the Venetians, Poles, Lithuanians, Mongols, and Turks.

The Angevin dynasty (1308–1382), which followed the Arpads on the throne, produced its most brilliant ruler in Louis the Great (1342–1382). Although he and his successors struggled valiantly with the inherited problems of the kingdom, they were severely limited by the failure of their fledgling cities to give them financial support. Hence, reduced to dependence on a levy of feudal cavalry for an army and on voluntary services of the nobility for a bureaucracy, Louis did what he could to help develop the monarchy. It is a testimony to his genius that in spite of the weakness of his position he was able to accomplish as much for Hungary as he did. Not only did he contribute to the prosperity of the country, but he also managed to sustain western cultural influences at his court and founded the first Hungarian university. Meanwhile, he inherited the Polish throne, subjugated the principalities of Wallachia and Moldavia, extended his power south into Bulgaria and Bosnia, and regained the Dalmatian coast.

Sigismund of Luxemburg, who eventually succeeded Louis on the Hungarian throne in 1387, became emperor in 1410 and king of Bohemia in 1436. Although he was an ambitious ruler, his aims and tastes exceeded his resources and ruined his ability to meet rapidly increasing responsibilities. For Sigismund and his subjects the fifteenth century may be said to have opened in 1389, when the Turks broke the resistance of the Southern Slavs at Kossovo. Not only did the Hungarians find themselves saddled with the burden of defending the Cross against the Crescent; they gradually discovered that they were involved in a struggle for survival which was to continue through most of the seventeenth century. Sigismund never succeeded in organizing an effective crusade against the Turks. First, because of the Venetians' morbid jealousy of Hungarian interests in Dalmatia, he could not persuade them to join him in a campaign against their common foe. Second, he himself could not resist the temptation to dissipate his energies by aiding the Teutonic Knights against the Poles or by organizing crusades against the Hussites.

Following Sigismund's death in 1437, the throne of Hungary remained an object of contention until the Polish king, Ladislas Jagello, won election by promising Polish troops to fight the Turks. In 1444 he and the prince of Transylvania, John Hunyadi, led their crusaders to a disastrous encounter with the infidels at Varna; Ladislas apparently earned the martyr's crown, although some believed he escaped to live out his life as a hermit. Hunyadi salvaged a remnant of the army, only to be beaten again in 1448, this time so definitively that Constantinople was left open to conquest by the Turks.

Undaunted, John Hunyadi assumed the regency of

Hungary and continued, with significant assistance from the Vlach principalities, to guard the Danube frontier. By saving Belgrade in 1456 and thus demonstrating that the Turks—and particularly their elite infantry, the Janissaries—were not invincible, he died a hero in 1457. His son and successor, Matthias Corvinus (1457–1490), managed to bridle the nobility and maintain Hungary's predominance in the Danube Basin. Although these achievements were accomplished mainly by the notorious Black Troop, an oversized bodyguard of mercenaries paid partly with plunder, this last Magyar sovereign made his court at Buda a brilliant center of culture. Though it reflected Hungary's revived power, it also exhibited the western orientation of its sovereign and the Italian influence of his Neapolitan wife, Beatrix.

Following Matthias' death in 1490, the nobility exploited the inevitable struggle for succession to exact concessions from the rival candidates. The king of Bohemia, Ladislas Jagello (1490–1516), in an effort to outbid the Hapsburg contender, promised to desist from the military adventures and to renounce the absolutist ambitions of his predecessors. He won the crown, but neither he nor his son Louis (1516–1526) was able to exercise the recently established powers of the monarchy. The realm was torn by intrigue, the outlying provinces fell away, and the possibility of organizing a common front against the Turks was frittered away. Even though members of the same dynasty now wore the three crowns of eastern Europe, the Jagellon kings of Poland-Lithuania had little interest in forging closer ties with their relatives in Bohemia and Hungary. The possibility of, as well as the need for, mutual aid ended in 1526, when Louis's followers were slaughtered by the Turks at Mohacs and he drowned trying to escape.

The western fringe of Hungary that was salvaged from that disaster went to the Hapsburgs, while some surviving native Magyar princes managed to maintain semi-independence in the buffer region of Transylvania. The long, oppressive Ottoman occupation (1526–1697) and the incessant raiding by Turks and Hapsburgs turned Hungary into a wasteland on which peasants eked out a miserable existence and the few remaining gentry cooperated with the Turks. Mediaeval Hungary lay in ruins, but its legend of heroic resistance to invaders from the east survived into the nineteenth and twentieth centuries to fire the minds of patriots.

Southeastern Europe

The history of the Turkish conquest of the Balkans begins in the high Middle Ages, when the traditional power in the peninsula was the Byzantine Empire. From the capital at Constantinople, the Byzantines ruled the Serbs and the Bulgars and campaigned against the Seljuk Turks for control of Asia Minor. During the thirteenth century the power structure in those areas was toppled by two dramatic events: the capture of Constantinople by Crusaders and the collapse of the Seljuks. The western feudal lords of the Fourth Crusade, who conquered Constantinople in 1204, divided the city, the Greek peninsula, and the Aegean Islands between themselves and their ally the republic of Venice. Three Greek pretenders set up rival states in other parts of the dismembered Empire, while the Serbs and the Bulgars asserted their independence. One of the Greek claimants, Michael Paleologus, reoccupied Constantinople in 1261 and founded a dynasty which was to last until 1453. But neither he nor any of his successors was ever able to reunite all the old Byzantine territories or to restore the former grandeur of the Empire.

Shortly after the Byzantine debacle of 1204, the degenerate Seljuk sultanate in Asia Minor, weakened by Mongol pressure, finally succumbed. One of its former mercenary generals, Osman (1259–1327), who had been stationed on the Greek frontier farthest from the Mongols and nearest to the Christians, began to lead razzias, or holy wars, against the Byzantines. The numerous recruits from various Turkish tribes who joined him in these popular forays came to be known as the Osmamlis, or Ottomans Turks. Under Osman's son and successor, Orkhan (1327–1362), they overran the western part of Asia Minor, which by then had been largely abandoned by the Mongols. But this was only a beginning.

Indefatigable warriors inspired by fanatical devotion to Islam, the Ottoman Turks became the greatest conquerors of the later Middle Ages. Asian nomads by origin, they were unsurpassed cavalrymen; and their famous Janissaries, a corps recruited from their Christian subjects and converted to Islam, gave them an elite infantry to match. Rigidly disciplined and prohibited from marrying, these magnificent troops were taught to regard the sultan as their father and the regiment as their family. The highest offices of the state were open to them, and they earned the reputation of being the world's best fighting force.

Although the Ottomans came from Asia, they achieved their most spectacular early successes in Europe. In 1354, they crossed the Dardanelles to begin the conquest of the Balkans, an objective which they would achieve a century later with the seizure of the ultimate prize, Constantinople, in 1453. Finding the Bulgars involved in fratricidal struggles with the Serbs, and the Greeks hopelessly divided among themselves, they defeated both in a series of battles before closing their vise on Constantinople. The now desperate Greek emperor appealed to the West for military aid to relieve his encircled capital; but the responding crusaders were overwhelmed by the Ottomans at Nicopolis in 1396.

Thus, on the eve of the fifteenth century Byzantium appeared to be at the mercy of the Turks. In 1402, however, the Ottomans were diverted from their prize by a crushing defeat at the hands of Tamerlane. With the sudden death of this formidable Tartar chieftain in 1405, his empire broke up almost as rapidly as it had been conquered, and the Turks were able by 1422 to return to their offensive against Constantinople. Though at first unsuccessful, they maintained the initiative and at Varna, in 1444, annihilated another force of western crusaders, that the Greek emperor had procured at the price of union with the Latin church. In 1453, Sultan Mohammed II (1451–1481) resumed the siege, this time with a highly developed plan backed by a fleet and massed artillery. For the second and last time in history the battlements were successfully stormed, and despite heroic resistance, Constantinople fell on May 29, 1453. With the city, Mohammed won the epithet "the Conqueror."

Even though Constantinople had long been a mere enclave in Turkish territory, its fall stunned Christendom. The impact on the West, however, was largely psychological, and only the papacy was seriously concerned with the recovery of the city. Nicholas V tried in vain to arouse Europe, and Pius II died heartbroken by his failure to launch a crusade.

The other consequences of the Turkish conquest of

the sacred capital were as varied as they were important.
Economically it helped the cynical Venetians, who continued to trade with the conquering Turks and profited
enormously as the price of grain from the plantations
along the southern shores of the Black Sea, as well as that
of spices and other eastern goods, rose sharply in the
West. Moreover, the economic advantage Venice now
enjoyed in the eastern Mediterranean incited ambitious
Genoese adventurers like Columbus and the Cabots to
seek new trade routes to the Orient. The fall of the city
also ended the brief union of the Catholic and Orthodox
churches; and by thus confirming the schism in Christendom, it offered a precedent to later Protestant reformers.
But though the fall had symbolic value, what we now
know of the long decline in wealth and population,
already suffered by the city in the preceding period, robs
the final collapse of political significance. The fate of one
city, however famous or strategic, could no longer deter-
mine the course of Europe's history.

The Ottomans quickly followed their triumph with the
occupation of the rest of Serbia and Greece. On land,
only the Magyars, Vlachs, and Albanians continued to
oppose their advance; but in the Mediterranean, they
were blocked by the Venetians and the Knights Hospital-
ers, an order of fighting monks who, after the fall of the
Holy Land in 1291, had retreated to the island of Rhodes.
Instead of smashing the opposition in Europe and the
Mediterranean, the Turks turned first to the south and
east, where they overran Armenia, Syria, and Egypt. Not
until the early sixteenth century did they return to the
offensive in the Danube Valley.

Constantinople, renamed Istanbul by its conquerors,
became the capital of their empire. In a sweeping admin-

istrative <u>reform, Mohammed placed each province under</u>
<u>a military governor called a bey, who was integrated into</u>
<u>a bureaucracy staffed largely by Greek civil servants.</u>
This hierarchy was headed by a <u>grand vizer,</u> or prime
minister, and two "beys of beys," one responsible for the
European and the other for the Asiatic provinces of the
Empire. Following earlier Persian and Arabic practice,
<u>Mohammed dealt with his new Christian subjects through</u>
<u>their religious leaders, thus conferring on the church an</u>
<u>increased authority and prestige that gave it an Oriental</u>
<u>character w</u>hich it was to retain long after its liberation. *millet system*
Any resistance to the Ottomans met with atrocious
reprisals, and Christians faced sporadic persecution.
Exactions were heavy, and the annual recruitment of boys
for the Janissaries and girls for the harems was degrading;
but the <u>Christians were little molested</u> in other ways.

While the Mongol legacy to the Russians was tyranny,
that of the Ottomans to the Balkans was poverty, igno-
rance, and humiliation. The Ottoman realm, even more
than that of Muscovy, remained an Oriental despotism
which had virtually nothing in common with the emerging European states.

Eastern Europe

It remains, finally, to consider the development of the
people whose state was gradually to absorb all of eastern
Europe. Although the <u>Russians</u>' role in the fifteenth century hardly presaged their later expansion, their history
in this period can now be seen to have contributed to their
remarkable development. Early in the thirteenth century,
Genghis Khan, leading a host of nomadic tribes loosely
referred to as Mongols or Tartars, had conquered most
of Siberia, all of Persia, and parts of China. Batu, Genghis'

grandson, inherited the western fourth of that huge empire, which he used as a base for a lightning conquest of European Russia. There he formed the great new khanate of the Golden Horde, ending the Kievan, or Varangian, period of Russian history. (See Sullivan, *Heirs of the Roman Empire*.) His despotic successors ruled southern Russia directly but supported semiautonomous Russian princes in the north and west in return for tribute in the form of men and taxes. In return for these abject services, the khans defended the princes against their own rebellious subjects or their European neighbors, particularly the Teutonic Knights. The princes of Moscow rivaled those of neighboring Tver as agents and beneficiaries of the ruthless Mongols.

During the second half of the fourteenth century, however, civil conflict within the Golden Horde laid Mongol territory open to attack. The Poles seized Galicia, while the Lithuanians occupied all of White Russia and a significant part of the Ukraine. Most of western Russia was thus freed from Mongol sway, and although its inhabitants remained Orthodox, they were, following the conversion of the Lithuanians, brought under western Catholic jurisdiction. Only the Great Russians remained under the Mongol yoke, and for another hundred years they continued to absorb Asiatic influences which today still distinguish them from their western neighbors.

Two centuries of Mongol domination cast a blight on Russia. Its once flourishing cities were demolished and their merchants and artisans scattered. The Ukrainian population was left prey to roving bands of Tartar raiders. Many survivors migrated and settled in the vast northern forests, where they constituted a sparse population consisting of a small group of aristocratic landowners, or boyars, and a mass of peasants, slaves, and serfs. Helpless, in any case, and conditioned to despotic rule by the khans, the Russian nobles accepted the absolutism of their own princes in return for aid in controlling the lower classes and resisting the invasions of Germans and Lithuanians. Thus, the Russian princes, salvaging abandoned Mongol institutions, continued the tyrannical abuse of the peasants long after the invaders had been driven out.

Religion and culture also felt the impact and retained the imprint of Mongol occupations. Prepared to tolerate any religion so long as it did not challenge their authority, the Mongols had left the Russian church to the close supervision of the native nobles who, by using it as an agency of control, turned it into the principal focus of Russian life. As a result, the peasants, most of whom had remained pagan during the Kievan period, now joined the upper and middle classes in accepting conversion. Churches and monasteries prospered and proliferated. Monks colonized the wilderness and, with the labor of peasant pioneers, cultivated it so successfully that many of the convents became fabulously rich. The consequent attachment of the peasants to the church (and of the church to wealth) long remained an outstanding characteristic of Russian life. But intense as were the religiosity and mysticism which permeated Russian culture during this period, the Russian church was not allowed to develop any institutional independence under the Mongols, with the result that it succumbed to the domination of Moscow as soon as the country was liberated from their occupation. In fact, this merely re-established the condition of state control that the Orthodox church had known under Kiev and Byzantium.

As international struggles weakened the Mongols in Muscovy, Grand Duke <u>Basil II (1425–1462)</u> managed to draw power into his own hands. Helped by an economic upswing, he and his successor were able, by the early sixteenth century, to realize their ambition of making Muscovy the most authoritarian state in Europe. Ivan III (1462–1505)—<u>Ivan the Great</u>—after affirming his independence from the Golden Horde, began expanding his hereditary holdings. In the sparsely settled eastern lands he met little opposition, and the movement he had begun continued unchecked through the great forests of the northeast until Russian pioneers ultimately reached the Pacific. In the southeast, Ivan succeeded in overrunning lands along the Volga and encouraged groups to push across the steppes beyond his frontiers, where they lived in constant dread of Tartar attacks, much as American settlers did of Indian raids. In this exposed position some, known as <u>Cossacks</u>, produced a vigorous, individualistic culture, which for centuries defied absorption by any great power.

Muscovite expansion into the long-settled and more heavily populated west, however, met strenuous resistance. Only after a hard campaign did Ivan succeed in subduing the proud and powerful princes of Tver and the prosperous commercial republic of Novgorod. By these conquests, particularly that of Novgorod, which derived its prosperity from the exchange of Russian forest products for Hansa wares, he finally brought Muscovy into important contact with the West. Aided by local uprisings, Ivan also began to dispute Lithuanian control of White Russia and the Ukraine and managed to seize several border districts of those provinces. Ever since, this Russian pressure toward the west and south, begun by Ivan, has remained one of the most constant and disturbing factors in European politics.

In the mid-fifteenth century the metropolitan of the Russian church asserted his independence from the Greek patriarch and, rejecting the Union of Florence (whereby the Byzantine emperor had agreed to subject the Orthodox church to the papacy in return for aid against the Turks), proclaimed Moscow the center of Orthodox Christianity. In 1472, Ivan III married the niece of the last Byzantine emperor and, on the basis of this and an earlier marriage, claimed the imperial inheritance and the title Tsar, or Caesar. Thus both church and state could assert that Moscow had now supplanted Constantinople, as that city had previously supplanted Rome. Since Ivan's day, Russian imperialism has often been inspired, consciously or unconsciously, by the conviction that Moscow was the "third Rome," the center of Orthodoxy, and the rightful capital of the world.

Summary

In summary, it appears that a fundamental economic lag in the countries of east-central and eastern Europe—with Muscovy providing a partial exception—largely prevented them from achieving the strength and unity of western states. The relative lack of trade, and consequently of towns, left the nobles and prelates with no effective rivals and deprived the princes of important allies. Without a source of revenues with which to hire loyal armies or efficient bureaucracies, royal resources were seriously restricted, and the position of the nobles was consequently strengthened. Able to refuse to pay taxes, they were free to subjugate the peasants, who could not appeal to royal agents. Split by religious, ethnic, and racial differences compounded by class hatreds, every kingdom was also vulnerable to invasion because of the absence of natural frontiers. The surprising thing is not that the great dynasties of east-central and eastern Europe failed to create solid national or princely states of the sort that was appearing in the West, but that they were able to acquire so much independent authority.

From the Battle of Mohacs until the eighteenth century, Poland, Bohemia, and Hungary gradually lost their hard-won independence to military invaders: the Russians, Ottomans, and Germans. Concurrently Catholicism was forced to retreat before the advance of Orthodoxy, Islam, and the new Protestant heresies. After 1500 the Western Slavs and the Magyars, who had experienced a golden age in the fourteenth and fifteenth centuries, entered a long period of stagnation from which they were to emerge only once—briefly, after 1918—before succumbing again to German and Russian domination. The Muscovite, Hapsburg, and Ottoman despotisms failed, however, to satisfy or assimilate the heterogeneous, impoverished masses under their sway. In 1917–1918, all three collapsed, after centuries of unmitigated misrule and oppression.

CHAPTER V

Ideas and Art～～～～～～～～～～～～

WHEN the magnificent edifice of mediaeval culture began to disintegrate early in the fourteenth century, many and diverse efforts were made either to shore it up or to replace it with something new. Realists and nominalists continued to define and elaborate the basic tenets of scholasticism, while other conservatives strove to maintain the old traditions in art and letters. At the same time, innovators began to question or even to reject traditional reason in favor of mysticism, heresy, naturalism, and skepticism. Subject to the buffeting and tempering of the socioeconomic upheavals that followed the Black Death, those intellectual movements that survived had, by the opening of the fifteenth century, been reorganized around four principal traditions, each with its own geographical focus. First, the still considerable remains of scholasticism were defended in the stronghold of the Paris-Dijon-Brussels triangle; second and less important, the mystical *devotio moderna* had taken root in the northern Netherlands and Rhenish Germany; third and of still more limited influence, the Hussite heresy persisted in Bohemia; and fourth and ultimately most significant, the early Renaissance was already illuminating Italy. Though each developed initially in relative isolation, increasing contacts and exchanges eventually bore fruit, during the last decade of the century, in the high Renaissance.

I.

Strongholds of Tradition

Custom, unquestionably the strongest cultural force at the beginning of the fifteenth century, maintained its sway until the end; and the great royal or ducal courts, such as those of France and Burgundy, and the older universities were its principal supporters. Political centralization (the concentration of power in monarchical or princely hands) and the growth of secular bourgeois society effectively undermined the authority of the aristocracy and clergy but oddly failed to challenge their cultural hegemony to anything like the same extent. Even while his military and economic pre-eminence was waning, the feudal noble—especially outside Italy—successfully defended his privileged position against the pretensions of the burghers and consequently set the tone of society and art.

Fifteenth-century literature north of the Alps clearly illustrates the tenacity of the chivalric tradition. Even the translations of such classical authors as Livy, Cicero, and Aristotle, sponsored by French kings and princes, were really paraphrases and adaptations designed to vaunt the hardiness, patriotism, and prowess of Roman "knights" as inspiring examples for contemporary warriors. Later, when the court of Burgundy superseded that of Paris as the center of chivalry, romances about knights of ancient Troy, Greece, and Rome took their place beside those about King Arthur as models for manners, education, and political action.

Assimilating mediaeval and contemporary influences

into their fanciful flight from reality, the most successful French and Burgundian poets reveled in archaic forms, mediaeval symbolism, courtly conventions, and florid rhetoric, thereby gaining the name *grands rhétoriqueurs*. Few writers of the period attempted to understand human psychology or to maintain any contact with daily life, but some did achieve a certain vigor and freshness: François Villon carried on the vagabond tradition, and Antoine de La Salle satirized, albeit sympathetically, the decadent chivalry he saw around him. A far greater number clung to the models of earlier generations, and the Englishmen John Lydgate and Thomas Occleve imitated the traditional elements of Chaucer rather than his innovations.

Even the introduction of printing did little at first to alter this literary trend; William Caxton, the first English printer, for example, published editions of Chaucer, devotional works, and translations of French romances. As late as the seventeenth century, Cervantes directed his satirical masterpiece *Don Quixote* against the long-popular chivalric romances of Spain.

Courtly traditions also dominated social forms. The elaborate ceremonial etiquette perfected by the dukes of Burgundy remained the model for emperors, kings, and princes for the next three hundred years. The ideal of courtly love, institutionalized earlier in the famous *cours d'amour*, became especially significant in the fifteenth century. Aristocrats set up such "courts" in order to judge delicate issues of conduct and to listen to recitations of troubadour poetry. The bourgeois counterparts of the *cours d'amour*, at least in the Burgundian areas, were the *chambres de rhétorique*, or *rederijkerskamers*, secular associations for the performance of miracle plays and the composition of rhetorical works. Similarly, the creation of new orders of chivalry, such as the Garter in England, the Golden Fleece in Burgundy, and the Saint-Michel in France, as well as the periodic calls issued by popes and monarchs for crusades against the Turks, manifested the continuing, if dwindling, influence of the chivalric ideal.

At the beginning of the fifteenth century the richly ornate International Style dominated painting and sculpture in most of Europe. Growing out of the High Gothic of Burgundy and northern France, it was characterized by decorative refinement, elaborate details, and intense emotional expression. Although sculpture, used to embellish the walls of buildings, long remained subordinate to architecture, painting began to emerge from its position as a minor art used in illuminating manuscripts. With the waning of French fortunes after Agincourt, artistic leadership shifted from Paris to the Burgundian court at Dijon and to the Netherlands. With the growing prosperity of the commercial towns of Flanders, bourgeois patrons were not only increasingly able to support the arts, but did so to a degree and with a discernment still apparent from the rich heritage of altarpieces and portraits in the churches of the area and the museums of the world.

One of the early Burgundian innovators was the sculptor Claus Sluter. Working at the turn of the fifteenth century in the service of Philip the Bold, he managed to eschew his native tradition of preciosity (the ingenious use of intricate detail) for a new dramatic immediacy. Without sacrificing grandeur or a sense of spatial freedom, his sculpture still caught essential reality in the vivid delineation of feature and costume.

The two leading Netherlandish painters of the century were Jan van Eyck and Roger van der Weyden. Van Eyck held the appointment of court painter to the duke of Burgundy; Van der Weyden became the official painter of the city of Brussels. But both enjoyed commissions from wealthy bourgeois and nobles as well. Like Sluter, Jan van Eyck synthesized descriptive details within simple shapes. His luminous colors, made possible in part by new oil paints, subtly recorded light to produce effects of stylized grandeur and spatial clarity. In Van Eyck's painting natural phenomena and everyday objects are used to provide complex references to mediaeval religious symbolism. Thus light as a symbol of divine presence shines in a burning candle or in the sun's rays passing through a window. Roger van der Weyden achieved comparable luminosity in his paintings, but with less emphasis on the details of physical setting and more on the subtleties of emotion. He used rhythmic organization of lines and contours to define figures, suggest movement, and highlight the depiction of surfaces and materials. The contributions of Jan van Eyck and Roger van der Weyden—the creation of the illusion of space and texture as functions of light and the expressive refinement of linear rhythm—exercised a dominant influence on much European painting during the fifteenth century. Only the Italians produced independent innovations of equivalent force, and even they reflected the impact of these Netherlandish developments.

In architecture, too, change was apparent. Though the great vertical Gothic continued to dominate cathedral construction in England, a new flamboyant style began to prevail on the Continent and even to extend its influence to the private palaces and public buildings commissioned by proliferating lay patrons—kings, nobles, and rich burghers. Such treasures as the town halls of the Netherlands and the residence of the French financier Jacques Coeur at Bourges exhibit the delicacy of décor that was characteristic of this new style and different from the monumental quality of earlier Gothic cathedrals and the organic simplicity of contemporaneous Italian buildings.

In the realm of learning, the universities, led by Paris, tended to remain international centers and purveyors of scholarly traditions. Their theologians continued to regard men as basically depraved, doomed by original sin to suffer the pains of purgatory if not the fires of hell. Theology still dominated the unchanged curricula, and controversies continued to rage among the disciples of Thomas Aquinas, Averroës, Duns Scotus, and William of Ockham. The scholastics had even scored what appeared to be a major triumph at the end of the fourteenth century when, following the failure of the clergy and lay rulers to resolve the papal schism, they proposed a conciliar solution. Such renowned scholars as Conrad of Gelnhausen, Henry of Langenstein, Pierre d'Ailly, and Jean de Gerson—all associated with the University of Paris—formulated a complex theory that won almost universal acceptance. Soon after the schism opened in 1378, Conrad had suggested, since canon law offered no solution for the crisis, an appeal to a power superior to the papacy and the cardinals, that is, a general council of the entire church, would be necessary. Both he and Henry of Langenstein then urged that either the king of France or some other appropriate authority convoke such an assembly; but their pleas went unheeded until, in 1391, Jean de Gerson finally persuaded the French clergy and crown to withhold obedience and support from the contending popes. The immediate effect of this organized resistance was to produce an independent Gallican church; but Gerson and his fellow nominalist Ailly persisted in their efforts to perfect a conciliar theory.

Recognizing that the church needed reform as much as reunification, they proclaimed a revolution in ecclesiastical government. Having first denied the divine origin of the pope's *plenitude potestatis* (full authority in spiritual and secular affairs), they then advocated the substitution of a representative, constitutional government for papal absolutism. Not even the most extreme partisans of the councils proposed to dismantle the monarchical structure of the papacy; they merely wanted to subject the Pope to the superior authority of the assembled representatives of Christendom. Moreover, revolutionary as this theory was in ecclesiastical affairs, it was hardly new as a concept of orderly and responsible government. For the Europe that had developed such legislative bodies as the cortes, diets, estates, and parliaments, every major precept of conciliar theory represented sound mediaeval tradition; the schoolmen were merely applying it to a new situation. In the end, councils did end the schisms; but because they failed to reform the church, their authority and prestige declined after the middle of the century.

Devotio Moderna

In the fifteenth century a new intense, self-conscious piety emerged among the inhabitants of the towns of the northern Netherlands and Rhenish Germany. Of distinctly bourgeois origins and having little connection with the main stream of mediaeval tradition, the so-called *devotio moderna* exercised relatively little influence outside this restricted area until the great Reformation of the sixteenth century. If the leaders of this spiritual revival owed much to the strand of mysticism which ran like a brilliant thread through the history of Christianity, they also put their own simple stamp on the movement. In the preceding century, for example, a series of German mystics, notably Meister Eckhart, Johann Tauler, Heinrich Suso, and the sect called Friends of God (see Lerner, *Age of Adversity*), inspired by such writers as John Scotus Erigena, Joachim of Floris, and even St. Bonaventura, had speculated freely in alarmingly heretical directions. The *devotio moderna*, disparaging such abstruse intellectual efforts, held that the essence of religion—spiritual communion with God—could be achieved only after an individual had freed himself from sin and made religion an integral part of his daily life. Hence, in place of theological abstractions it emphasized piety, morality, and work.

Gerard Groote (1300–1384), the founder of the *devotio*, was born in the little Dutch town of Deventer and educated at Paris, Prague, and Cologne. Returning to the Netherlands, he won a popular following as a preaching deacon; but his fervent attacks on clerical worldliness prompted the hierarchy to revoke his license in 1383. As a result, he withdrew to Deventer, where, surrounded by a small group of disciples, he formed a devotional brotherhood, later to be known as the Brethren of the Common Life. Soon, similar *fraterhuizen*, as these semimonastic communities for men or women were called, began to form in one city after another. While the brothers and sisters of the Common Life, mostly laymen, were not bound by formal monastic vows, they lived by strict self-

imposed rules and supported their charitable and educa-
tional work largely by copying manuscripts.

As educators the Brethren excelled. Consecrating a
major part of their energies to the religious training of
boys, they established, or came to control, some two
hundred schools scattered through the Netherlands and
adjacent regions of Germany. Hostile to scholastic methods, they welcomed the new humanist learning from
Italy and early utilized the printing press. In their most
famous institution, the school at Deventer, the Brethren
developed the most advanced curricula and pedagogy
north of the Alps. The impact of their efforts on the
intellectual developments of the time can be suggested
by the fact that from their student body of about two
thousand boys came some of the most illustrious authors
of the age—including Rodolphus Agricola, Jean de
Gerson, Nicholas of Cusa, Thomas à Kempis, and
Desiderius Erasmus.

One branch of the Brethren regularized its status by
joining the Order of Canons Regular of St. Augustine
and founding its own monastery at Windesheim. In time
other groups, inspired by the piety and devotion of this
model, adopted the same rule, until by the end of the
century, the Windesheim congregation numbered nearly
a hundred houses and effected the most important
monastic reforms of the century. Although some clerics
opposed the *devotio moderna*, it was tolerated by most
ecclesiastical authorities so long as its adherents eschewed
heresy and violence.

One of the most famous and widely read works of
Christian piety to appear in this period—*The Imitation
of Christ*—was inspired by the *devotio moderna*. Probably composed by Thomas à Kempis of St. Agnes, a house

of the Windesheim congregation, the *Imitation* stresses neither dogma nor doctrine. Rather, it is a devotional work in the strictest sense, aiming to prepare the individual through purification and faith for spiritual communion with God. Arguing that this could not be achieved by intellection, Thomas emphasized morality and mystical understanding, rather than philosophical speculation: "I had rather feel compunction," he insisted, "than know its definition." Similarly, he advised constant inner purification, frequent reading and contemplation of Scripture, performance of good works, and regular Holy Communion as the requisites for religious fulfillment.

The *devotio moderna* inaugurated a fundamental shift in European religious orientation. Though they never broached criticism of established doctrine, its advocates nonetheless constituted a subtle threat to the church. Their concern with ethics and their propensity for ignoring philosophical speculation tended to reduce the importance of formal theology. Likewise, their preoccupation with the inner spirit and with direct individual union with God personalized piety but also laicized religion by minimizing the significance of the sacraments and the clergy. Full as it was of promise for the church, the *devotio* also carried implicit threats, which were later realized in its inspiration of leaders of both the Protestant and Catholic Reformations.

The Hussite Movement

To the east of Germany, in Prague, John Hus (1369–1416) initiated another great intellectual movement. Despite a tendency to violence, it resembled the *devotio* in being urban, popular, pietistic, and limited to a specific geographic region. Its origins can be traced to the efforts of the Luxemburger kings, who were also Holy Roman emperors, to make Prague one of the cultural, as well as political, capitals of Europe. (See above, Chapter IV.) Quite inadvertently, their success fostered the development of a sense of Czech identity and an increased restiveness with German domination. In 1391 two pious citizens of Prague endowed the Bethlehem Chapel to provide sermons in the Czech language and to encourage vigilance against clerical corruption. But since the clergy in Bohemia was under German domination, such demands for church reform inevitably carried nationalist overtones, as was tragically demonstrated when, in 1402, John Hus was appointed to the pulpit.

The most famous Czech in history, Hus was already a leader among the masters at the University of Prague, where he had won his own Master of Arts degree and become a champion of realism against the nominalism favored by the German majority of the faculty. In disputations, he defended John Wycliffe's unorthodox opinion that the church consisted of all persons predestined to salvation, but he stopped short of the Englishman's denial of the real presence of the blood and the body in the Eucharist. Thus Hus's doctrines, while not technically heretical, nonetheless constituted a dangerous challenge to the spirit of the established church.

In his preaching, too, he trod dangerous ground. Stirring as much opposition throughout Europe as enthusiasm in his own congregation, he called upon Christians to support neither of the rival popes; and he provoked widespread controversies by his attacks on the growing corruption and immorality of the clergy. Inveighing not merely against the abusive traffic in indulgences, Hus also began to question such common practices as tithing. He denounced the exercise of secular power by churchmen, particularly the so-called crusades proclaimed by popes against their political opponents, and reminded the faithful that they were not bound to obey papal commands that conflicted with the law of Christ.

The radical character of his theses, the violence of his language, and his immense popularity won Hus the animosity of the ecclesiastical establishment. It was not surprising, therefore, that he should be excommunicated by the archbishop of Prague in 1409 and that this act should irreparably split the clergy in Bohemia. In a desperate effort to restore religious peace the Emperor, Sigismund, persuaded Hus to go before the newly convened Council of Constance in 1414 to defend his position. There, in spite of his imperial safe conduct, his enemies won the upper hand. Having begun by condemning Wycliffe's works and ordering his bones exhumed and cast out of consecrated ground, the assembled fathers were in no mood to deal lightly with Wycliffe's chief defender. The Council condemned Hus as a heretic and then, in accord with canon law but in violation of Sigismund's personal guarantees, ordered him turned over to the Emperor to be burned at the stake.

The resulting fury of the Hussites plunged the country into civil religious war; but their campaign against both Pope and Emperor was partially dissipated by their own internal divisions. A radical group called Taborites split from the moderate majority, provoking a bloody internal struggle. By 1436, however, the moderates had re-established control of the movement and decided to seek reconciliation with Rome. They offered to respect the Pope's supremacy in return for certain concessions, particularly the right of the laity to participate in the

Communion in "both kinds," that is, to partake of the wine as well as the bread—a practice which suggested their names: Utraquist, meaning "both," and Calixtine, from the chalice for the wine. Although the Pope agreed, the settlement proved fully satisfactory to neither side, and remained largely inoperative. The Utraquists maintained what was at best an uneasy relationship with Rome until, a century later, they chose individually between Catholicism and Lutheranism; and the remnants of the Taborites went their own way, rejecting transubstantiation, denying the existence of purgatory, condemning the veneration of relics, and electing their own priests. They were unrepentant forerunners of the Protestant Reformation, in which they would eventually merge.

By the end of the century, destructive wars, shifts in trade routes, and the transfer of imperial interest and activity to the West, reduced Prague to a provincial capital and Bohemia to a troubled backwater. But the Hussite movement had not only put both intellectual and political ideas into action, but it had also wedded two of the most potent forces in modern history. Hus had launched a heroic campaign on behalf of the liberty of individual conscience and another for the freedom of national self-expression. As a result, he had unleashed explosive forces that would carry the reformers of the next century much farther than he himself had been able, or for that matter would have been willing, to go.

New Developments in Italy

The occasional flashes of intellectual and artistic innovation in northern Europe were completely outshone by the cultural blaze in Italy. There, a small elite generated

an intense new interest in classical antiquity and initiated
a brilliant new style in art. Singly, each of these achievements constituted a revolutionary technical development;
combined, they created a profoundly secular vision of
man that directly assaulted the whole traditional value
structure based on uncompromising asceticism and
defended by abstract theology, to replace it with a
dynamic and potentially cataclysmic faith in man and
nature that came to be known as humanism. This Renaissance mystique—though largely confined to an intellectual elite—was powerful enough not only to transform
Western culture and, by extension, to reshape the world
but to maintain its prestige virtually unchallenged in
educated and influential circles until the twentieth
century.

   In spite of their revolutionary impact, however, these
" Renaissance men of fifteenth-century Italy had far less
intention of creating something new than of reviving
 something old." Accordingly, they failed to follow important new paths in natural science opened by the fourteenth-century scholastics; indeed, they tended to disdain
speculation altogether, priding themselves, rather, on
their studied imitation of antiquity. But despite their
professed intent to revive the classical tradition of pagan
Greece and Rome, they interpreted their antique models
in the light of their Christian heritage. This combination
of mediaeval attitudes and classical models—two indis-
putably conservative sources—proved to be radical in
fusion; and however retrospective their aims, the Italians
produced a new culture.

   Renaissance humanists achieved far more than a mere
revival of Greek and Latin literature. Mediaeval literati,
who had always enjoyed a wide acquaintance with the

classics, had, during the twelfth century, recovered a considerable number of previously lost writings, including Latin translations of a substantial part of the Aristotelian corpus. In the course of the thirteenth and fourteenth centuries more and more scholars encountered these manuscripts as texts in schools and universities. Italian scholars of the *quattrocento* (the fifteenth century) infused their work with a new dedication to the Ciceronian ideal of *humanitas*: the conviction that the individual human personality, with its unique dignity, should be developed to its full potential. Further, the humanists believed, as their predecessors had not, that by pursuing the perfection of man and nature they could create a new, superior culture. Indeed, they coined the term "Middle Ages" to describe pejoratively the long period separating their era, which they regarded as a period of cultural rebirth, from the glorious past of Greece and Rome. Their program of *studia humanitatis* led them to develop their understanding of philology, to systematize the search for lost manuscripts, and to pursue the study of the language and the recovery of the literature of ancient Greece.

The fourteenth-century Italian scholar Francesco Petrarch (1304–1374) fathered humanism as a result of consciously undertaking to master all the Latin classics. During his reading, he found frequent references to works no longer known; he inferred that they must have been mislaid and forgotten, perhaps forever lost. But in the hope that some might still exist, even if only in a few imperfect manuscripts hidden away in recesses of monastic libraries, he left his privileged position at the rich and cultured papal court of Avignon to set out on a systematic and astonishingly successful search for missing masterpieces. At Liège he discovered two of Cicero's speeches, and at Verona, where a copyist had recently turned up the works of Catullus, he found letters from Cicero to Atticus, Quintus, and Brutus. His enthusiasm turned to passion, and his success touched off a craze for hunting "lost" literary works as well as ancient coins, inscriptions, and *objets d'art*.

Petrarch inspired the Florentine Giovanni Boccaccio (1313–1375) to follow his example of collecting and studying the classics. The author of the famous *Decameron* uncovered works by Ovid, Martial, and Ausonius, and assisted in recovering Varro and substantial portions of the *Histories* and *Annals* of Tacitus. With the encouragement of Petrarch, Boccaccio set out to become indeed, as he believed he was, the first western European scholar to read Greek since Scotus Erigena in the ninth century.

After the deaths of Petrarch and Boccaccio, other Florentine scholars, including Coluccio Salutati, Niccolò de' Niccoli, Poggio Bracciolini, and Leonardo Bruni, carried on their work. Among Poggio's finds, which though spectacular in themselves were representative of the group, were works by Cicero and Tacitus, not to mention less spectacular texts of Quintilian, Lucretius, Ammianus Marcellinus, Petronius, and Plautus. By the middle of the fifteenth century, the major portion of retrievable Latin literature, including most of its masterpieces, had been salvaged by the humanists.

In 1396 the civic authorities of Florence persuaded Manuel Chrysoloras of Constantinople to come to their city to teach Greek. Although his presence may have kindled more enthusiasm than actual scholarship, Greek studies were to receive significant impetus from the

Council of Ferrara-Florence that met from 1437 to 1439 to plan the reunion of the eastern and western churches. The exposure of the more than five hundred Orthodox delegates, many of whom were learned scholars, to the West seems to have contributed to the increasing immigration of Byzantine intellectuals to Italy during the next decade. The result of this influx was both to stimulate interest in Greek literature and to guide its study. The émigré scholars also brought rich collections of classical manuscripts, initiating a profitable traffic in which even the papacy became involved. Thus, contrary to a once widely held view, when Constantinople fell to the Turks in 1453, much of Greek literature had already found a refuge in Italy, but even if that disaster did not precipitate the westward flight of scholars and books, it did help to complete the movement.

The revival of Greek learning renewed a long-dormant interest in Plato. One of the Greek representatives at the Council of Ferrara-Florence, Gemistus Plethon, reopened an ancient controversy by a series of lectures on the philosophical superiority of Plato to Aristotle. European scholastics immediately rallied to the defense of their "Philosopher" and the Aristotelian-Thomistic tradition. Cosimo de' Medici, on the other side, provided a villa near Careggi and an endowment that enabled Marsilio Ficino (1433–1499) to spend the rest of his life translating and interpreting the works of Plato. The Villa Careggi attracted such outstanding intellects as Pico della Mirandola, the young genius who introduced the study of Hebrew to the Christian West, and Politian, the brilliant scholar and poet who drew students to Florence from as far away as England and Germany. Ficino's informal circle which became known as the Platonic Academy, served as a prototype for the development of similar societies, first in other Italian cities and eventually throughout Europe, to disseminate the new humanistic learning that was so unwelcome in the universities. This impassioned love of Plato had an impact on philosophy and science that began to change the basic outlook of educated Europeans on aesthetics, education, history, politics, and eventually religion—thus inaugurating attitudes which still prevail today.

Humanists' efforts to understand the ancient world produced more literary scholarship than original literature. In order to use the materials they had unearthed, they elaborated philological rules and techniques, compiled grammars and lexicons, and composed guides to, and commentaries on, ancient works. They imitated classical authors in a vast outpouring of elegant, if artificial, Latin works. Their slavish efforts to assimilate their ancient models tended to retard the development of the vernacular literature that had made such a promising beginning in the fourteenth century, until interest in that literature was finally revived in the later fifteenth century and reaped the benefits of the feeling for structure, form, and style awakened by the humanists.

Prompted by their new competence in textual criticism, the humanists began to question an increasing number of the traditional assumptions and conclusions of mediaeval scholarship. A particularly brilliant and important example of textual analysis was provided by Lorenzo Valla's famous and elegant demonstration that the "Donation of Constantine," the document by which the emperor Constantine had supposedly given the western half of the Empire to the papacy, was a forgery. It is not without significance that Valla subsequently became a papal secretary and a canon of the Lateran Church.

Later Niccolò Machiavelli (1469–1527) applied the principles gleaned from his own analysis of Roman history entitled *Discourses on Livy* to his *History of Florence* and, in *The Prince*, to the ruthless politics of his own day. He demonstrated that the attitudes of the strong new monarchs deviated even more strikingly than their conduct from the mediaeval ideal of a Christian prince. Brushing aside the threadbare pieties that exhorted rulers to practice Christian virtue and respect the rights of their subjects, Machiavelli described and analyzed the conduct of government as he observed it. The modern state, he explained, subordinated all lesser corporations, persons, offices, and laws to its perpetual quest for greater security and power. The sovereign, he argued, whether assembly, prince, or king, judged and legislated with absolute authority. Thus, using Italian and classical models, Machiavelli brilliantly dissected the operations of the modern state, but nearly two hundred years were to elapse before others would dare confirm the accuracy of his insights or attempt to justify his doctrine of political amorality. No matter how their monarchs behaved, men were slow to alter their views on the purpose and nature of government.

Inevitably, the cult of *humanitas* produced a new outlook on life and especially on education. As the century progressed, Renaissance man, armed with borrowed classical urbanity and a historical view of his inheritance, began to turn against the mediaeval ideal of the monastic life. Rejoicing in his natural endowments and capacities, he vaunted human ambition, pride, and passion. *Virtù*, a combination of personal ability and effrontery, became his byword. Multifarious accomplishments, including a facility for taking advantage of any situation, became his highest goal. Such "universal" men as Leonardo da Vinci

and Leon Battista Alberti, each an accomplished diplo-
mat, scientist, engineer, inventor, athlete, and artist—
and, in consequence, rich and famous—became models
of Renaissance men.

Art in the *quattrocento* reflected many of the same
humanistic interests and attitudes. Examples of ancient
art had always been accessible in Italy, and since the late
thirteenth century a growing number of artists in the
Tuscan towns of Pisa, Florence, and Siena had drawn
inspiration from the beauty, dignity, and solid physical
presence of figures in Roman sculptural remains. This
trend was not merely developed but was also transmuted
by the incomparable genius of Giotto. The great Florentine painted human figures of such palpable substance
that observers were said to feel able to reach out and
touch them. By the middle of the century, however, there
was a pronounced reaction against the human ideal in art.
Possibly a product of the Black Death and the subsequent
socioeconomic dislocations, this new mood found expression in the rigidly hieratic, remote, and abstract two-
dimensional representation of religious images. Only at
the beginning of the fifteenth century did the severity of
this dehumanized style yield to the courtly grace and
sparkling detail of what came to be known as the International Style. An even more important development began
with a group of Florentine painters who saw themselves
both as followers of Giotto and as revivers of antiquity.
By stressing clarity, rational organization, and harmonious proportion, they launched what was to become
famous as the Renaissance style in Italian art.

Although the imitation of ancient classical models was
only one, perhaps even minor, aspect of the Florentine
Renaissance, certain intellectual principles believed to

derive from antiquity profoundly influenced the new art. Both Christianity and Neo-platonism taught that the bodily proportions of man, who had been created in the image of God, mirrored the perfection and harmony of the universe. The *De architectura* of Vitruvius, the only ancient treatise on tectonics to survive, interpreted the base, shaft, and capital of classical columns in terms of the human body; and Leonardo da Vinci revived the concept by sketching man's body within, and conforming to, various geometrical figures. (See the frontispiece.) Renaissance architects made the diameter of a column the basic unit of measurement for all the dimensions of an edifice. By working with multiples or even fractions of that unit, they believed they could weld the parts of any building into an organic and harmonious whole directly related to man. Similarly, painters developed a new system for determining linear perspective comparable to the column module in architecture. This scheme, by placing the vanishing point directly opposite the spectator's eye, makes all dimensions and distances, spatial volumes and spatial intervals, measurable in terms of the height of a man's eye above the ground. Many fifteenth-century painters and sculptors, as well as architects, explored complex spatial relations with this rationalizing device, thus demonstrating the overriding Renaissance concern with man as the ultimate point of reference of human thought and expression.

The greatest architects of the century were Filippo Brunelleschi, Leon Battista Alberti, and Donato Bramante. Brunelleschi's masterpiece, the cathedral of Florence, with its classic dome, not only provided a dramatic contrast to the soaring spires and perpendicular lines of the Gothic of the north but created an entirely new Renaissance style for Italian churches. Leon Battista Alberti, mathematician, scholar, poet, and jurist, established his great reputation as an architect with such magnificent buildings as the Rucellai palace in Florence and with the first incunabulum treatise on architecture. And Bramante, commissioned by Pope Julius II, began the rebuilding of St. Peter's Basilica in 1503. Although his designs were repeatedly altered by those who carried on the task after his death, it is his great dome that still gives the building its majestic character.

The same preoccupation with three-dimensional mass can also be seen in painting. In contrast with their northern contemporary Jan van Eyck, who made light interact with a variety of surface textures, the Florentine painters used it to evoke powerful shapes and figures and to suggest the light-diffusing atmosphere in the spatial intervals between them. From about the middle of the fifteenth century, however, as the work of Netherlandish painters became better known in Italy, Florentine studies in the use of light showed the impact of their influence.

While some were pursuing the rationalization of space perception, the sculptor Donato Donatello and the painter Masaccio were developing an analytical approach to the expressive potentialities of the human figure. Less concerned with anatomical detail than were their successors after 1450, these artists placed more emphasis on the basic structural relations, particularly the balance between weights and stresses among the main parts of the human body. The effect was both the creation of monumental rounded forms and the revelation of the shifts and adjustments of weight around the body's axis. The same emphases are evident in the generalized, structurally articulated nude figures of Masaccio's *Expulsion from Eden* and Donatello's *David*.

An extraordinary number of distinguished artists worked in Florence during the fifteenth century—Fra Angelico, Fra Filippo Lippi, Paolo Uccello, Ghirlandaio, Sandro Botticelli, Andrea Mantegna, and Perugino, for example—though few achieved the grandeur of Masaccio or the expressive range of Donatello. Only Michelangelo Buonarroti matched these great innovators; in his work the art of the Renaissance reached its spectacular triumph. Scion of an old aristocratic family, Michelangelo poured his turbulent genius into poetry, painting, architecture, and above all, monumental sculpture. The marble of his *David*, *Moses*, and several pietàs glows with spiritual intensity. These figures, which he strove to "free" from the stone, achieve a grand but poignant humanity with their heroic pride and pathos.

Assimilation and High Renaissance

Four cultural forces—the mediaeval tradition, the *devotio moderna*, the Hussite heresy, and the Italian Renaissance—merged or clashed with increasing intensity as the fifteenth century drew to its close. The major humanistic influences flowed north from Italy to scholars who, by adapting the new attitudes and techniques to their own interests and needs, produced what is sometimes called "Christian humanism." Although its religious complexion separated Christian humanism from the predominantly secular humanism of contemporary Italy, some ideas from the North made the return trip and were absorbed in the South; and similar exchanges occurred between East and West, across the Continent—from England to Bohemia and Hungary and back to Germany.

At first peripatetic scholars, professors, and students acted as the principal purveyors of these intellectual commodities. The schools recently established by the

Brethren of the Common Life and the new universities in Germany became important centers for the exchange and dissemination of ideas. Artists proved to be effective carriers of innovations in style and technique as they roamed over Europe. Church councils, diplomatic missions, and fairs provided additional opportunities for intellectuals to meet. After mid-century, however, the invention of printing revolutionized the transmission and dissemination of ideas and transformed scholarship and education as well, first by making texts readily and widely available, and second by so reducing their cost as to make them accessible to a much larger public. Movable type, developed about 1450 by Johann Gutenberg of Mainz, arrived in France in 1470, in Hungary in 1473, in England in 1475, and in Florence in 1477. Thus, by the end of the century the printed word was bringing a widening circle of Europeans together in ever closer and more significant communication.

By mid-century even French universities, among the most conservative in Europe, reflected the new influences from Italy by the introduction of humanistic Latin grammars and the importation of a few teachers of Greek. The Sorbonne actually set up a press to print the new works. Innovations, however, had a greater impact after Charles VIII invaded Italy in 1494. A genuine lover of art and literature, Charles actively supported the importation of Renaissance culture to France, setting a precedent by bringing back works of art, establishing a colony of twenty-one Italian architects and master craftsmen, and urging provincial universities to adopt the new curricula. Progress was slow, but during the last decade of the century two French humanists, Jacques Lefèvre d'Etaples and Guillaume Budé, not only won great acclaim as scholars but succeeded in reorienting French intellectual life. The critical biblical studies of the former established him as his country's first significant reformer, while the works on Greek language and literature earned for the latter his title of "Wonder of France."

In England, Humphrey, duke of Gloucester, himself a friend of many of the humanists, early began to collect a classical library and to send protégés to Italy to study. Gradually Italian humanists and even a few Greeks made return visits to England, but such exchanges remained sporadic during the fifteenth century. Later, William Grocyn, Thomas Linacre, and John Colet studied in Italy under the masters Politian and Ficino, much to the benefit of English humanism. A spirit akin to that of the *devotio moderna* moved all three theologians to apply humanism to the problems of religious understanding and reform.

The prosperous southern towns of Germany, especially Nuremberg, Augsburg, and Ulm, had long been in close commercial contact with Italy. It is hardly surprising, therefore, that they were aware of the new learning and were sending students to Italian universities. Also, recently established universities such as Basel (founded in 1460), less steeped in scholastic tradition than Paris and Oxford, were more open to the humanistic ideas and techniques they received from Italy. The best known names in German humanism are Rodolphus Agricola and Johann Reuchlin. Agricola, famous for his teaching as well as his accomplishments in music and the arts, became Germany's "universal man," while Reuchlin, a former student of Pico della Mirandola and a master of both Greek and Hebrew, was Germany's outstanding reformer at the beginning of the sixteenth century. Significantly, Agricola and Reuchlin both received their early schooling from the Brethren of the Common Life at Deventer.

Indeed the new school at Deventer became the single

most important source of new ideas, not merely in the Netherlands but throughout the North. From the beginning the Brethren encouraged the critical study both of the Latin classics and the Bible, using humanist grammars and texts in their classes even though they did not fully accept the spirit of humanism until the end of the century. But so thorough was their training that one of their students, Nicholas of Cusa (1400–1464), eventually became the most celebrated intellectual in northern Europe. Though neither strictly nominalist nor realist, he speculated on the metaphysical problems that had occupied the scholastics for centuries, and at the same time applied the new techniques of critical analysis to scientific and textual problems. He blended elements of Eckhartian mysticism and the *devotio moderna* with Platonic concepts to form his own highly personal philosophy. Emulating the example set by Italian humanists, he searched diligently for manuscripts, finding among other things twelve plays of Plautus. As the result of a developing interest in natural science, he drew the first reasonably accurate map of central Europe and offered hypotheses about the motion of the earth and the nature of the universe that anticipated the great formulations of Copernicus. He also took an active role in church affairs, becoming first a bishop and eventually a cardinal-legate. Always an advocate of reform, he championed the conciliar movement and then supported the reinstated papacy. With widespread and varied contacts, Nicholas of Cusa was in a position to assimilate elements from all areas of Europe and to develop a broad and tolerant eclecticism.

Italy, the indisputable fountain of Renaissance art and letters, also made important contributions to the devel-

opment of a new style in taste and manners that would
influence the rest of Europe. Although the old social dis-
tinctions between the nobility and the bourgeoisie had
largely disappeared in Italy by the fourteenth century,
the rise of such families as the Sforza, the Este, the
Gonzaga, and the Montefeltro during the fifteenth initiated an aristocratic revival. The new princely courts
conferred titles and patronized the arts in much the
manner of the Franco-Burgundian model. Even the traditional republics like Venice, Florence, and Bologna
were influenced by the new trend; and the Medici were
far from being the only citizens of a republic to assume
airs of nobility. Chivalry flowered once again as tales of
knighthood from old court literature were revived to
elaborate and illustrate the new social ideal: the perfect
courtier. The specifications for this flawless knight and
"universal man" were given their classic formulation by
Baldassare Castiglione in his gentleman's handbook,
Il Cortegiano (*The Courtier*), which significantly became one of the most widely read works of the Renaissance.

The generation that drew inspiration for its courtly
society from the North went to the same source to renew
its spiritual and religious beliefs. As a group, Italian
humanists never rejected Christianity but merely
eschewed traditional piety for a more secular outlook,
stressing such diverse but worldly interests as literary
taste and civic virtue. Toward the end of the century,
however, many of them—notably Ficino and Pico—
plunged into metaphysical speculation and theological
argument. Influenced by Plato's emphasis on both the
ethical responsibility and the mystical resources of the
individual, they found much to admire and share in

the moral and devotional spirit of their northern contemporaries.

Only with this development did the new learning become meaningful to the scholars of northern Europe. Because of their religious orientation, the secular literature of antiquity had concerned them very little. Hitherto they had followed the work of their Italian colleagues mainly to acquire improved techniques for handling Latin and Greek. As the Italians finally began to deal substantively with religious texts and problems, however, they caught the eager attention of such northern scholars as Colet, Lefèvre d'Etaples, and Reuchlin, all of whom drew important inspiration from their work. The new Platonism provided the intellectual preparation that nourished the religious reformations of the following century and, at the same time, initiated the search for a truly European synthesis of philosophy, literature, art, and science.

This pattern of North-South interchange and assimilation finds a graphic reflection in the work of three artists: the Italians Leonardo da Vinci and Raphael Sanzio, and the German Albrecht Dürer. In the early part of the fifteenth century, Italian artists borrowed many innovations from their colleagues in the Netherlands, but toward 1500 the current had reversed and northerners had begun to seek new ideas in Italy. Leonardo was a pivotal figure in this exchange, profoundly influencing Raphael and Dürer, as well as his own countrymen Michelangelo and Bramante. He was working in Milan when the French took the city, and after much urging went to France, carrying his new ideas with him. He had early developed an obsessive commitment to the pursuit of artistic perfection and devoted years to the close empirical study of nature and human anatomy. An intellectual as well as an artist, he studied optics to learn more about the principles of light and color, collected biological specimens, experimented with new pigments, dissected bodies to understand their structure, and filled volumes of notebooks with detailed sketches of what he had observed. In addition to mastering proportion and perspective, he learned to capture mood and emotion in the meticulous representation of his models. Careful attention to arrangement, posture, facial expression, gesture, and shading infused his work with a new psychological perception of human nature. The fame of his great *Last Supper*, for example, derives quite as much from its unsurpassed revelation of character and emotion, to which all details contribute, as from its technical perfection.

Raphael and Dürer present the fascinating contrast of a northern and a southern artist assimilating the influence of Leonardo. Though their personalities and careers differed significantly, they were both conceited, self-centered, "universal" men. Raphael, a major architect as well as a great painter, had a peculiar gift for discovering and absorbing the spirit of his time. Dürer, widely traveled and well informed, also made contact with many leaders of his profession, including Leonardo's circle in Milan, though not Leonardo himself. Although he worked in nearly every medium, Dürer attained his greatest fame with woodcuts and engravings, and like Raphael is best known for his religious subjects. In spite of superficial differences, their works have much in common. Dürer probably created the first complete fusion of northern emotion with Italian formalism; and Raphael succeeded in imbuing his religious subjects with both idealized and human qualities. Although in strikingly different ways, each man achieved a tone that escaped the stereotypes of either mediaeval religious painting or early Renaissance realism. While Dürer's small engravings approach the heroic, Raphael's magnificent frescoes breathe the intimate. Both artists projected into their representations of man and the world a vital and compelling force derived not merely from their precise rendering of nature, but also from their penetration into the mystery of existence. Creating figures that seem to move of their own inner necessity, they depicted man as they believed him to be—the image of God.

Epilogue ‿‿‿‿‿‿‿‿‿‿‿‿‿‿‿‿

THE historical concept of the Renaissance as it was developed and celebrated by Jakob Burckhardt and his followers contains a paradox that derives from the contradiction between the conscious aims and ambitions of the men of the fifteenth century and later appreciations of their accomplishments. What historians have taken to be a brilliant series of revolutionary innovations was originally undertaken in a self-conscious and determined effort to recapture the past. The great humanists, artists, rulers, and adventurers of the period, that is, had their eyes turned, not on the future generations who would acclaim them, but on the lost heritage of their ancient predecessors. Consequently, the immediate fruits of their labors were all retrospective: a keenly renewed interest in the study of history and mythology, the revival of classic forms of art and literature, the restoration of the unity of the church and the purity of sacred texts, the revival of feudal government and chivalrous society, and the recovery of prosperity and economic security.

Hoping to bolster or replace the tottering traditions of mediaeval culture, Renaissance intellectuals and artists set out to recapture what they considered the lost moral and intellectual grandeur of the classical past. Instead, they often handed on to posterity—unwittingly as well as unintentionally—new and revolutionary ideas and attitudes. In their efforts to resurrect old concepts of governance, both clerical scholars in the employ of church councils and lay publicists in the service of new princes adumbrated much of the modern theory of political secularism and constitutionalism. Architects, sculptors, and painters were led, through their imitation of classical models, to new discoveries in techniques and design. At the same time, by their intensive study of the works of Livy and Polybius, historians developed a modern historical perspective and political science.

The inherent contradiction is strikingly illustrated by the intentions and achievements of Niccolò Machiavelli and Christopher Columbus. No two men better represent the spirit of the Renaissance—Machiavelli as an intellectual, humanist, and critic, Columbus as an adventurer, courtier, and discoverer. *The Prince*, perhaps more than any other single work, epitomizes the demystified realism taken by so many historians as the hallmark of Renaissance thought. But even if he is credited with inventing modern politics, Machiavelli's emotional commitment was to ancient Rome. He is said to have worn a toga as he worked in his study, and he seriously advocated the revival of the weapons and tactics of the Roman legion at a time when cannons were making their appearance on the field of battle. Similarly Columbus, whose discovery of the New World surely must be regarded as the greatest achievement of the age, not only had not dreamed of making a discovery, but failed even to realize what he had accomplished. Instead, he had hoped to restore

Genoa's lost commercial primacy by opening a new, shorter ocean route to the Orient and, incidentally, to rediscover legendary kingdoms long believed lost to European travelers. Thus, the two men of the Renaissance who may have made the greatest contributions to the world we know were concerned exclusively with reviving the glories of the past.

In every field, efforts to restore and preserve the old led inadvertently but inevitably to startling and unexpected discoveries. Although, for the men of the Renaissance, their most important accomplishment was the recovery of Greek and Latin classics, the real significance of this achievement was not, as its authors supposed, the development of a fuller understanding of the past. Instead, because the study of pagan antiquity sparked parallel efforts to re-evaluate early Christian literature, its results included the religious reformations and the wars of the following centuries, as well as the eventual triumph of toleration and secularism with which they ended. The humanists also recovered the scientific works of the ancients, opening the way to the scientific revolution of the seventeenth century. The Renaissance humanists, in short, effected a catalysis in the western intellectual tradition that was to go far beyond their aims or ambitions.

Perhaps more important was the expansion of horizons caused by Renaissance discoveries. Though Columbus and his captains found neither the lost kingdoms nor the easy passage to India they sought, they proved that the ocean sea was conquerable and stumbled upon an unknown world. Their exploits furnished unprecedented riches for their European monarchs and opened literally unlimited new prospects that led almost immediately to the exploration and colonization of the distant coasts of the New World. By the eighteenth century Europeans had turned the Atlantic into an enormous "Mediterranean," and by the nineteenth their oceanic civilization encompassed the entire globe.

By accelerating an already growing awareness of man as not merely a terrestrial being but as one capable of mastering his world, the recoveries and the discoveries produced a secular outlook and concern that would bequeath to subsequent centuries the impetus to alleviate suffering, oppression, and injustice in human society.

Long before they undertook voyages across uncharted seas, Europeans had begun reconstruction at home. In despair over the chaos accompanying their failure to make feudalism, or feudal monarchy, work, some elements of European society began to give their support, more or less grudgingly, to strong princes and the centralized states they were beginning to create. Untrammeled personal authority, increasingly supported by a growing sense of common national purpose, proved to be the only force—as Machiavelli had seemed to argue—capable of imposing order on, and providing security for, Europe's turbulent population. New absolute monarchies that embodied his concept would culminate centuries later in nation states, but they first emerged in the Renaissance.

Among the chief supporters of the new dynasties were the bourgeoisie, members of a new socioeconomic class who were also just beginning to exert their full political influence. Taking advantage of new types of land contracts, improved credit facilities, and advances in technology, these men, few in number at first, were destined—at least in western Europe—to become a dominant class of capitalist entrepreneurs directing the expansion of

European commerce overseas and, eventually, the development of our modern industrial economy.

Without the new confidence engendered by the humanists' affirmation of the worth of man and the world, and without the new opportunities for economic exploitation in the Americas, Africa, and Asia, however, the Renaissance innovations in technology, business, statecraft, art, and letters could probably not have been supported on such a lavish scale. Like the recurrent renaissances and reform movements of the Middle Ages, they might well have run a limited course and perished. But with a wholly new orientation and a new and unprecedented source of economic support, they were not only to survive but to alter the course of history. Recovery led first to a restoration of lost values but then inadvertently to the innovation and expansion which both separated the modern from all preceding cultures and established the civilization of western Europe as the model for the entire world.

Chronological Summary

1384–1398	Jadwiga, "king" of Poland
1385–1402	Gian Galeazzo Visconti, duke of Milan
1386–1434	Jagello, Grand Duke of Lithuania, converted, married Jadwiga, and became king of Poland, joining the two realms
1396	Manuel Chrysoloras came to Florence
1398–1430	Vitold, Grand Duke of Lithuania
1399	Richard II, king of England, deposed and died
1399–1413	Henry IV, king of England
1400	Wenceslas deposed as Holy Roman Emperor
1400–1464	Nicholas of Cusa
1401–1428	Masaccio
1402	John Hus began preaching in Prague
1404–1419	John the Fearless, duke of Burgundy
1406–1454	John II, king of Castile
1409	Council of Pisa and election of a third pope; Hus became rector of the University of Prague
1410–1437	Sigismund, Holy Roman Emperor
1413–1422	Henry V, king of England
1414–1417	Council of Constance
1415	Execution of Hus; Battle of Agincourt
1419–1467	Philip the Good, duke of Burgundy
1420	Emergence of Taborites among the Hussites
1422–1461	Henry VI, king of England (and claimant to France); Charles VII, king of France
1425–1462	Basil II, Grand Duke of Muscovy
1429	Joan of Arc raised siege of Orléans
1431	Joan of Arc burned at stake at Rouen
1433–1499	Marsilio Ficino
1434	Cosimo de' Medici assumed control of Florence after exile
1434–1444	Ladislas III, king of Poland
1435–1442	Sigismund, king of Bohemia
1438	Pragmatic Sanction of Bourges
1438–1439	Council of Ferrara-Florence; Albert of Hapsburg, Holy Roman Emperor

1439	Union of eastern and western churches
1439–1493	Frederick III, Holy Roman Emperor
1440–1444	Ladislas, king of Poland, elected king of Hungary
1442	Alfonso of Aragon conquered Naples
1445	Platonic Academy established in Florence
1446–1452	John Hunyadi, regent of Hungary
1447–1455	Nicholas V, Pope
ca. 1450	Printing invented
1450–1466	Francesco Sforza, duke of Milan
ca. 1450–ca. 1500	Population growth, economic prosperity, political and social stability; new universities established in northern Europe
1451–1481	Mohammed II, Sultan of the Ottoman Empire
1452–1519	Leonardo da Vinci
1453	Hundred Years' War ended; Ottomans captured Constantinople
1454	Peace of Lodi; Wars of the Roses began in England
1454–1466	War between Poland and Teutonic Knights
1454–1474	Henry IV, king of Castile
1457–1490	Matthias Corvinus, king of Hungary
1458–1471	George Podiebrad, king of Bohemia
1458–1479	John II, king of Aragon and Sicily
1458–1494	Ferrante I, king of Naples
1461–1483	Louis XI, king of France; Edward IV, king of England
1462–1505	Ivan the Great, Grand Duke of Muscovy
1464–1469	Piero de' Medici in control of Florence
1467–1477	Charles the Bold, duke of Burgundy
1469	Marriage of Ferdinand and Isabella
1469–1492	Lorenzo de' Medici in control of Florence
1469–1527	Niccolò Machiavelli
1470	Printing introduced in France
1470–1471	Henry VI restored to throne of England
1471–1516	Ladislas, king of Bohemia
1471–1528	Albrecht Dürer

1473	Printing introduced in Hungary
1474	Printing introduced in England
1474–1504	Isabella, queen of Castile
1475–1564	Michelangelo Buonarroti
1476–1500	Ludovico (*il Moro*) Sforza, duke of Milan
1477	Defeat and death of Charles the Bold at Nancy and marriage of Mary of Burgundy to Maximilian of Hapsburg; printing introduced in Florence
1477–1482	Mary, duchess of Burgundy
1479–1516	Ferdinand, king of Aragon
1483	Edward V, king of England
1483–1485	Richard III, king of England
1483–1520	Raphael Sanzio
1485–1509	Henry VII, king of England
1490–1516	Ladislas, king of Bohemia and Hungary
1492	Columbus discovered America; Lorenzo de' Medici died; Alexander V elected Pope; Granada reconquered, and Jews expelled from Spain; Erasmus ordained as priest
1493–1519	Maximilian, Holy Roman Emperor
1494	Ferrante, king of Naples, died, and French invaded Italy; Treaty of Tordesillas divided newly discovered lands between Spain and Portugal
1494–1498	Medici expelled from Florence, and Savonarola assumed control
1494–1529	Italian Wars
1497	Exploration of North American coast by John Cabot
1498	Vasco da Gama reached Calicut
1498–1515	Louis XII, king of France
1512	Medici re-established in Florence; Pacific Ocean discovered
1516–1526	Louis Jagello, king of Bohemia and Hungary
1526	Battle of Mohacs (Hungary fell to the Ottomans)

Suggestions for Further Reading⁓

THE best treatment of the "question of the Renaissance" is Wallace K. Ferguson, *The Renaissance in Historical Thought: Five Centuries of Interpretation* (Boston, 1948). The student will also find three problem books helpful: Karl H. Dannenfeldt, ed., *The Renaissance, Medieval or Modern?* (Boston, 1959); Denys Hay, ed., *The Renaissance Debate* (New York, 1965); and Werner L. Gundersheimer, ed., *The Italian Renaissance* (Englewood Cliffs, N.J., 1965).

The most important general works covering the fifteenth century include two recent texts, both spanning several centuries: an interpretative essay by Wallace K. Ferguson, *Europe in Transition, 1300–1520* (Boston, 1962), and an encyclopedic narrative by Samuel H. Thomson, *Europe in Renaissance and Reformation* (New York, 1963). The major volume in English devoted to the fifteenth century is the venerable *Cambridge Medieval History*, VIII: *The Close of the Middle Ages* (Cambridge, Eng., 1936), C. W. Previté-Orton and Z. N. Brooke, eds. There are two volumes covering the period in the lighter American counterpart, the Langer series: Edward P. Cheyney's *The Dawn of a New Era, 1250–1453* (New York, 1936), rather old-fashioned but well written, and the selective work by Myron P. Gilmore, *The World of Humanism, 1453–1517* (New York, 1952). Two volumes in the Methuen series are useful: William T. Waugh, *A History of Europe from 1378 to 1494* (London, 1951), and Arthur J. Grant, *History of Europe from 1494–1610* (2d ed., rev.; London, 1938). All the above works contain ample bibliographies. The first volume of the *New Cambridge Modern History: The Renaissance, 1493–1520* (Cambridge, Eng., 1957), edited by G. R. Potter, contains penetrating essays but no bibliography. A seminal work is Fernand Braudel's *La Méditerranée et le monde méditerranéen à l'époque de Philippe II* (2d ed., rev.; Paris, 1966), which focuses on that sea as the geographical foundation of European civilization.

Several volumes in the present series deal with aspects of fifteenth-century Europe: Robert E. Lerner's *The Age of Adversity: the Fourteenth Century* (Ithaca, N.Y., 1968), Marshall W. Baldwin's *The Mediaeval Church* (Ithaca, 1953), and Charles E. Nowell's *The Great Discoveries and the First Colonial Empires* (Ithaca, 1954) relieve the present volume of heavy responsibilities.

Social and economic history, a rapidly developing field, is more dependent than most on periodical literature, the bulk of it in foreign languages. The only major nonperiodical multi-volume series covering the period is John H. Clapham *et al.*, eds., *The Cambridge Economic History of Europe from the Decline of the Roman Empire* (3 vols.; Cambridge, 1942——). Jacques Heers, *L'Occident aux XIVᵉ et XVᵉ siècles: Aspects économiques et sociaux* (Paris, 1963), is an excellent brief synthesis.

The following are useful studies of special topics and areas. Classic treatments are the appropriate volumes of Mandell Creighton, *A History of the Papacy during the Period of the Reformation* (London, 1882–1894), and Ludwig Pastor, *History of the Popes from the Close of the Middle Ages, 1305–1799* (40 vols.; trans. from Ger.; London, 1936–1961). More readable are Alexander C. Flick, *The Decline of the Medieval Church* (2 vols.; London, 1930), and Walter Ullmann, *The*

Origins of the Great Schism: A Study in Fourteenth Century Ecclesiastical History (Hamden, Conn., 1967). The best treatment of the origins of modern diplomacy is Garrett Mattingly, *Renaissance Diplomacy* (Boston, 1955). On the Medici see Cecilia M. Ady, *Lorenzo dei Medici and Renaissance Italy* (London, 1955; and Collier Books paperback), Raymond A. de Roover, *The Rise and Decline of the Medici Bank, 1397–1494* (Cambridge, Mass., 1963; and Norton paperback), and Ferdinand Schevill, *History of Florence from the Founding of the City through the Renaissance* (New York, 1961). Gene A. Brucker, *Renaissance Florence* (New York, 1969), represents a new approach, focusing on the city itself. Geoffrey Barraclough, *The Origins of Modern Germany* (2d ed., rev.; Oxford, 1947; and Capricorn paperback), gives a fine description of late mediaeval Germany and may well be complemented with Samuel H. Thomson, *Czechoslovakia in European History* (2d ed.; Princeton, 1953). Richard Vaughan, *Philip the Bold: The Formation of the Burgundian State* (Cambridge, Mass., 1962), Otto Cartellieri, *The Court of Burgundy* (New York, 1929), and Joseph L. A. Calmette, *The Golden Age of Burgundy: The Magnificent Dukes and Their Courts* (trans. from Fr.; New York, 1963), describe that duchy's formation and glories. Volume I of Roger B. Merriman, *The Rise of the Spanish Empire in the Old World and in the New* (New York, 1918), remains the most useful and easily available English work on Spanish history for this period.

The involvement of France and England in the Hundred Years' War is best treated in Edouard Perroy, *The Hundred Years War* (trans. from Fr.; Bloomington, Indiana, 1959; and Capricorn paperback), which is well complemented by Henry S. Lucas, *The Low Countries and the Hundred Years' War, 1326–1347* (Ann Arbor, Mich., 1929). Works on Joan of Arc vary greatly: Joseph Calmette, *Jeanne d'Arc* (Paris, 1947), is balanced; Lucien Fabre, *Joan of Arc* (trans. from Fr.; New York, 1954), is hagiography; and Anatole France, *The Life of*

Joan of Arc (2 vols.; trans. from Fr.; New York, 1926), is critical. Pierre H. J. B. Champion, *Louis XI* (trans. from Fr.; New York, 1929), and John S. C. Bridge, *A History of France from the Death of Louis XI* (Oxford, 1921–1936), are both good treatments of France. The basic works on fifteenth-century England are volumes in the *Oxford History of England*: Ernest F. Jacob, *The Fifteenth Century, 1399–1485* (VI; Oxford, 1961); and John D. Mackie, *The Earlier Tudors, 1485–1558* (III; Oxford, 1961). See also the excellent analysis by Stanley B. Chrimes, *English Constitutional Ideas in the Fifteenth Century* (Cambridge, Eng., 1936). Particularly helpful to the student are two problem books: Arthur J. Slavin, ed., *The New Monarchies and Representative Assemblies: Medieval Constitutionalism or Modern Absolutism?* (Boston, 1964), and Gerald P. Bodet, ed., *Early English Parliaments: High Courts, Royal Councils, or Representative Assemblies?* (Boston, 1968).

Few works on east-central and eastern Europe are available in English, and most of them are heavily nationalistic in tone. The biased but useful survey by Oskar Halecki, *Borderlands of Western Civilization: A History of East Central Europe* (New York, 1952), should be read in conjunction with the critical and provocative synthesis by William H. McNeill, *Europe's Steppe Frontier, 1500–1800* (Chicago, 1964). See George Vernadsky, *A History of Russia* (5th ed.; New Haven, 1961; and Yale University Press paperback), and the much needed pioneering synthesis in social and economic history by Jerome Blum, *Lord and Peasant in Russia from the Ninth to the Nineteenth Century* (Princeton, 1961; and Atheneum paperback). For individual countries and areas see the following: William F. Reddaway *et al.*, eds., *The Cambridge History of Poland, I: From the Origins to Sobieski* (to 1696) (Cambridge, Eng., 1950); Otakar Odložilík, *The Hussite King: Bohemia in European Affairs, 1440–1471* (New Brunswick, N.J., 1965); Frederick G. Heymann, *George of Bohemia: King of*

Heretics (Princeton, 1965); Carlile A. Macartney, *Hungary: A Short History* (Edinburgh, 1962); Robert W. Seton-Watson, *A History of the Roumanians from Roman Times to the Completion of Unity* (Cambridge, Eng., 1934); Leften S. Stavrianos, *The Balkans since 1453* (New York, 1961); William E. D. Allen, *The Ukraine* (Cambridge, Eng., 1941); and Paul Coles, *The Ottoman Impact on Europe, 1350–1699* (London, 1968; and Harcourt, Brace and World paperback). The history of Hungary, the Balkans, and Turkey in this period is best treated in recent works on Byzantium or the Crusades: *Cambridge Medieval History, IV: The Byzantine Empire* (Cambridge, 1966), Joan M. Hussey, ed.; Sir Steven Runciman, *The Fall of Constantinople, 1453* (Cambridge, Eng., 1965); Kenneth M. Setton, gen. ed., *A History of the Crusades* (2 vols.; Philadelphia, 1955——); and Steven Runciman, *A History of the Crusades* (3 vols.; Cambridge, Eng., 1954; and Torch paperback). An older work by Carl Brockelmann, *History of the Islamic Peoples* (New York, 1961; and Capricorn paperback), is still useful for the Ottomans.

Ideas and art are the most written about aspects of the fifteenth century. The classic treatment of the continuing mediaeval tradition is Johan Huizinga, *The Waning of the Middle Ages: A Study of the Forms of Life, Thought and Art in France and the Netherlands in the XIVth and XVth Centuries* (trans. from Dutch; New York, 1960; and Anchor paperback). Also standard are Raymond L. Kilgour, *The Decline of Chivalry* (Cambridge, Mass., 1937); Annie Abram, *Social England in the Fifteenth Century* (London, 1909); and Brian Tierney, *Foundations of the Conciliar Theory: The Contribution of the Medieval Canonists from Gratian to the Great Schism* (Cambridge, Eng., 1955). A recent pathfinding work is Heiko A. Oberman, *The Harvest of Medieval Theology: Gabriel Biel and Late Medieval Nominalism* (Cambridge, Mass., 1963). On neoscholasticism see Meyrich H. Carré, *Realists and Nominalists* (Oxford, 1946). On the *devotio moderna* see Albert Hyma, *The Christian Renaissance: A History of the "Devotio Moderna"* (2d ed.; Hamden, Conn., 1965), and his *Brethren of the Common Life* (Grand Rapids, Mich., 1950), as well as Rudolf Steiner, *Mystics of the Renaissance and Their Relation to Modern Thought* (trans. from Ger.; New York, 1911), and Ernst Troeltsch, *The Social Teaching of the Christian Churches* (2 vols.; trans. from Ger.; New York, 1949; and Torch paperback). Among the newer and best works on the Hussite movement are Matthew Spinka, *John Hus and the Czech Reform* (Chicago, 1941), and Frederick G. Heymann, *John Žižka and the Hussite Revolution* (Princeton, 1955).

A very brief introduction to humanism is Frederick B. Artz, *Renaissance Humanism, 1300–1550* (Kent, Ohio, 1966). Basic works are Hans Baron, *The Crisis of the Early Italian Renaissance: Civic Humanism and Republican Liberty in an Age of Classicism and Tyranny* (2 vols.; Princeton, 1955; and Princeton University Press paperback); R. R. Bolgar, *The Classical Heritage and Its Beneficiaries* (Cambridge, Eng., 1954); Paul O. Kristeller, *The Classics and Renaissance Thought* (Cambridge, Mass., 1955); Roberto Weiss, *Humanism in England during the Fifteenth Century* (2d ed.; Oxford, 1957); Margaret M. Phillips, *Erasmus and the Northern Renaissance* (London, 1949; and Collier paperback); Henry Bett, *Nicholas of Cusa* (London, 1932); Nesca A. Robb, *The Neoplatonism of the Italian Renaissance* (London, 1935); and Eugene F. Rice, Jr., *The Renaissance Idea of Wisdom* (Cambridge, Mass., 1958). The standard work tracing the history of classical manuscripts and texts is John E. Sandys, *A History of Classical Scholarship* (3 vols.; 2d ed.; New York, 1958).

For Renaissance art see the following: Lionello Venturi and Rosabianca Skira-Venturi, *Italian Painting: The Creators of the Renaissance* (Geneva, 1950), and *Italian Painting: The Renaissance* (Geneva, 1951), both in the Skira series. Also see Bernhard Berenson, *The Italian Painters of the Renaissance* (2 vols.; New York, 1952; and Phaidon Press paperback); Millard

Meiss, *Painting in Florence and Siena after the Black Death* (Princeton, 1951; and Torch paperback); Erwin Panofsky, *Studies in Iconology: Humanistic Themes in the Art of the Renaissance* (New York, 1939; and Torch paperback); John Pope-Hennessey, *An Introduction to Italian Sculpture*, II: *Italian Renaissance Sculpture* (New York, 1958); Rudolf Wittkower, *Architectural Principles in the Age of Humanism* (3d ed.; London, 1962); Otto Benesch, *The Art of the Renaissance in Northern Europe: Its Relation to the Contemporary Spiritual and Intellectual Movements* (rev. ed.; London, 1965); Wilhelm Waetzoldt, *Dürer and His Times* (trans. from Ger.; New York, 1950); Oskar Fischel, *Raphael* (2 vols.; trans. from Ger.; London, 1948); and Kenneth M. Clark, *Leonardo da Vinci: An Account of His Development as An Artist* (rev. ed.; New York, 1963).

Index ~~~~~~~~~~~~~~~~~~~~~~~~~~~~~~~~